LURE FISHING

GW00669648

LURE FISHING
A New Approach to Spinning

Mike Ladle and Harry Casey

A & C Black · London

First published 1988 by
A & C Black (Publishers) Limited
35 Bedford Row, London WC1R 4JH

© *1988 Mike Ladle and Harry Casey*

ISBN 0 7136 5654 9

British Library Cataloguing in Publication Data
Ladle, Mike
Lure fishing: a new approach to spinning
1. Spin-fishing 2. Fishing lures
I. Title II. Casey, Harry
799.1'2 SH449

ISBN 0-7136-5654-9

Printed and bound in Great Britain by
Anchor Brendon Ltd, Tiptree, Essex

CONTENTS

INTRODUCTION

Three things are certain.

First, we are not rich; consequently most of our angling takes place on waters which are fished by quite a few other people.

Second, we are not armchair anglers; our long discussions about fishing usually take place on the river bank or sea shore.

Third, we are very critical and difficult to convince; manufacturers' claims and journalists' jargon do not impress us and it is only fish on the bank that count.

Our attitude to spinning with artificial lures is very simple, involving the minimum of swivels, traces, weights and other paraphernalia. Nevertheless we are never averse to trying out new techniques or lures and if a novel idea produces results it is developed; if it is found wanting, its weakness is considered and possibly modified. If there is an obvious fundamental flaw it is quickly rejected.

Mostly, on angling matters we think alike, but our long friendship makes it possible for us to exchange rude comments about each other's fishing tackle and technique without risk of a breaking off of diplomatic relations. In our case the give and take of deadly insult is part of the learning process – for in spite of our joint angling experience of over eighty years (we started *very* young!) many questions remain unanswered. Nor is our experience limited to angling in U.K. waters, for we have fished in many parts of the world.

In our first book, *Operation Sea Angler*, we described the two hundred or so hours which we spent each year sea-fishing. Following its publication we have often been asked what we do with the rest of our time; in *Lure Fishing: A New Approach to Spinning* we offer at least a part of the answer. On the banks of lakes, ponds or rivers we can be found "fishing quietly away", as Harry would put it, our methods ranging from natural bait fishing to spinning and fly fishing with artificial lures. Perhaps the best introduction to our basic approach is contained in the following recent experience.

One Sunday in early October we set out on what was intended to be a bass fishing trip, but on arrival we found conditions that were much too rough for us to fish our chosen beach. After a hasty cliff-top discussion we decided to abandon our first intention and to take advantage of a couple of free tickets (trout closed season) allowing us to coarse fish on a stretch of fly-only trout river. We turned our car inland and our thoughts to pike and perch.

On arrival, a lugubrious bailiff informed us that the trout season had produced nothing of outstanding interest. "The biggest brownie was two and three-quarter pounds and that was on mayfly. In fact, we've not had a fish over three pounds for a couple of years," he said, and added "If you're spinning, don't forget to use lures longer than five inches, so that you don't catch too many trout."

At the waterside we were disappointed and slightly annoyed to find that, despite the recent lack of rain, the water was the colour of strong, milky coffee. The construction of a new weir and bypass system was, through a recently dug channel, feeding chalky, clay-loaded water directly into the main stream.

"Oh, well. Since we're here, let's give it a go!" said Mike, and cast his large Mepps-Mino across the mouth of the new cut. The big spinning blade, bright though it was, could scarcely be seen at a depth of 6 inches – but no sooner had it begun to turn than bang! A fish was on. It was hardly a match for the bass tackle (carp rod, fixed spool reel and 8-pound line) and a $1\frac{1}{2}$-pound perch was swiftly brought to the net. Meanwhile, Harry was already into a second perch, and so it continued with fish up to $2\frac{1}{2}$ pounds following in quick succession. Then, suddenly, Harry's rod arched over as a much larger fish took the lure and set off downstream. Mike waited patiently with the net as the fish was worked towards the bank. As it turned, just below the surface, we saw the green and gold flank of an 8-pound pike. When it was netted and slid ashore Harry unhooked the pike and retied the lure as a precaution against damaged line.

Cheered by his success, Mike strolled along the bank and cast into the slightly clearer water of the adjacent mill stream. Within very few minutes his reel buzzed as a fish took line; it was now Harry's turn to wield the net, lifting out the largest chalk stream brown trout either of us had ever set eyes on – a monster of at least 5 pounds. It was carefully unhooked and slid back into the river. In spite of our big lures and our subsequent attempts to avoid "trouty" water, in the course of the day we landed eleven more brown trout, not one of them under 2 pounds. In addition, our total catch included twenty big perch, three small jack pike and five larger ones up to just about double figures. Harry even had a bonus grayling.

What a day to remember!

Acknowledgements
We wish to thank all our fishing companions who have shared their ideas and experience with us over the years.

Our thanks are also due to our excellent typist, Di Morton, and to our employer, the Freshwater Biological Association.

CHAPTER ONE

BEGINNER'S LUCK

It is only when you try to tell an inexperienced angler how to set about catching a particular type of fish that you realise just how much is involved. To make a decent catch is not quite as easy as it may seem to the experienced hand.

The whole business of experience and inexperience was put into perspective for us by an incident which happened a while back. Mike was beginning to have slight pangs of conscience combined with not a little curiosity, for Pete had already been down on the river for three hours and, although he said that he had "done a bit of fishing" before, perhaps Mike should have made more of an effort than simply to point him at the water. The idea of Pete's visit was to try and catch a salmon from our local river Frome. It was early March and the river was pretty full, so Mike had advised him to try a devon minnow.

As it turned out "devon minnow" to Pete meant metal-cylinder-with-fins, of which he had several in his bag. Not surprisingly the heavy devons caught everything but fish. Every cast raked up some fresh item from the river bed and, after losing two or three of the lures on snags, Pete decided that the advice had been worthless and changed to a Toby spoon.

Unaware of these events Mike pulled on his wellies, donned a warm coat, and set off to track down the budding salmon angler. It was not many minutes before he saw a figure standing by the big tree growing on the inside of "willow tree bend". As he approached it became clear that

Pete was "into something"; in fact, from his attitude and the steep curve of the rod in his hand, it was clearly something of large size. Mike broke into a trot and quickly covered the hundred yards or so to where his protégé stood, locked in combat. "How big is it?" he asked.

"Oh, about twenty pounds," came the casual reply. "It's my biggest so far."

"So far! You don't mean that you've had another?"

Mike could not believe his ears. He craned forwards over the marginal reed bed to obtain a better view and, as he did so, a great green torpedo hove into view. "But it's a pike," Mike said, with more than a hint of disappointment in his voice.

"Yes, I've had six of 'em," said Pete. "Bugger the salmon. I'd rather catch these!"

Now no one appreciates the appeal of pike more than Mike, and Pete's command of language suggests that he has the potential to be a competent angler. But the puzzling aspect of Pete's success was the fact that rarely did any of the other salmon anglers fishing the water catch more than an occasional pike. Why was it then that Pete, a comparative novice, was pulling them out like mackerel? To cut a long story short it turned out that, being unfamiliar with the well known preference of *Salmo salar* for a brisk flow of water, Pete had been fishing the slacker current on the inside of each bend of the river. In the slower flow, the lure which he was using wobbled and fluttered along just above the river bed, a method tailor-made to attract and catch pike. His success was entirely accidental.

In contrast to this, a friend of ours recently decided to take up spinning for bass. At the beginning of the year he bought a decent secondhand rod and reel – actually the gear on which Harry had caught many bass, pike and salmon in the past. His lures were shop-bought, high quality plugs of the type which we have shown over the years to be highly effective in catching fish. As we write this, in mid-July, he is still waiting to get his first bite.

In the following chapters we show how a wide variety of game, coarse and sea fish can be caught by spinning.

CHAPTER TWO

GIVE SPINNING A GO

The pros and cons of spinning

Why write another book about "spinning"? Many competent anglers have had a go at this subject, most of them adopting the same procedure. They list as many different lures as possible and speculate (at best, on the basis of personal experience; at worst, on information gleaned elsewhere) which of those lures are most appropriate for particular species of fish. This sort of treatment has been applied to all branches of our sport – coarse, game and sea.

As far as possible we have tried to break this mould and work from basic principles. To start with, it would be foolish to claim that the use of spinning tactics is *always* the best way of catching fish. No one would believe us and the results speak for themselves.

It is certain that if you adopt the principles and methods outlined in the following pages

1 you will catch fish,
2 you will enjoy exciting sport,
3 you will often catch more and bigger fish than many of your contemporaries who stick to more conventional methods.

Having said that, let us make it clear that no method or technique is "all powerful", so be prepared to switch to bait or fly when reason suggests that these methods will work better under the prevailing conditions.

Spinning – a second-class method

In many parts of the world the use of artificial lures is the standard method of fishing. Why? The traditional coarse fishing tactics are designed to catch the plant- or insect-eating fish so abundant in our rivers and lakes. The feeding habits of these fish seem to make the widespread use of spinning tactics for their capture quite unsuitable, much greater numbers and weights of fish being taken by the tried and trusted methods. This gives us our first clue. For a method to be widely accepted it has to be SUCCESSFUL. However "artistic" or "aesthetically satisfying" the use of a particular tackle or tactic is *supposed* to be, it MUST CATCH FISH. In practice, it must catch fish as well as, or better than, the methods which have been developed over centuries of trial and error. It is a fact that many British anglers have no faith in artificial lures.

Is it possible that our waters (perhaps because of their limited extent) have a smaller variety of predatory fish than those of other countries? In north American fresh waters, for example, there are several species of trout and pike, walleyes, two species of black bass, white bass, perch, charr, a number of sea-run trout and no less than eight species of salmon. Some of these fish have such strong predatory instincts that the novice will have the encouragement of frequent catches even during his first experiments with lure fishing.

On the other hand, in cold Scandinavian waters the variety of freshwater and marine fish is more restricted than in our Gulf Stream-influenced area. Nevertheless, spinning is still the basis of much of their angling. Part of the difference may be due to the relative absence of coarse fish, other than pike and perch, from the more acid waters of Norway and Sweden.

In complete contrast, most fishing in Britain involves various forms of float-fishing or bottom-fishing with edible bait. Only in salmon angling and, more recently, in deep-water wreck fishing for cod, pollack and coalfish, has the deep-seated mistrust of spinning tactics and lures been widely overcome. Small but enthusiastic groups of pike, trout, bass or mackerel "spinners" come and go with the fashions of the day, but the basic domination of bait fishing persists.

Are British fishes less "game" than those in African, Swedish or north American waters? Of course not; our predators, like all others, have to be swift, powerful and sure if they are to survive. Just watch and wonder next time a pike hurtles towards your lure or bait. Now you see it, now you don't!

It seems most likely that the reasons for lack of interest in spinning tactics are historical rather than logical. Richard Walker touched on the matter when he said that "every other way of catching trout [than fly fishing] is frowned upon and often forbidden". This attitude has, unquestionably, been an important factor in keeping spinning tackle and tactics in the doldrums. The prejudice has spread to salmon fishing, where it is often suggested that fly fishing is, in some mysterious way, superior to other methods. We are not opposed to fly fishing tactics in any way, but it is surely common sense to use the method that best suits the conditions. Our fishing time is limited, and consequently very precious, and when we go fishing we see no reason to handicap ourselves by adopting an inefficient approach.

The advantages of modern tackle

In fact, until the advent of the modern fixed-spool and multiplying reels and the development of fine, supple and strong nylon lines, it was not easy to "spin-fish" at all. In most circumstances fly fishing may well have been the most effective (and least clumsy) method of presenting an *artificial lure, at distance,* to predatory fish. This was highlighted for us in a comment by F.D. Holcombe in 1921. He wrote, "A very interesting method of catching bass is to cast a light spinning bait for them ... from the shore; but before he can accomplish this of course the novice will have to become *proficient in casting a light bait.*" A little later he says, "Long casting is generally necessary to success, and naturally the finer the line the farther one can cast with it; but *it must be strong enough to play a vigorous 4 lb or 5 lb bass ...*" He then goes on to talk about casting *over 40 yards* and using *1½oz of lead* on *8 lb line.*

Today it is quite possible for a novice or a youngster to cast unweighted lures seventy or eighty yards on tackle easily capable of landing the biggest bass that swims.

When spinning first became a practical proposition for everyone it was virtually outlawed by British game fishermen and, as a result, lures and tackle were never readily available. Because of this obstructive attitude there was no incentive for manufacturers to develop the market.

An American viewpoint

In North America there were less preconceived ideas about the acceptability of methods and, in the absence of private waters and unhampered by restrictions, spinning was seen for what it is – an extremely productive, enjoyable and exciting way of fishing for a wide range of fish. The American angler, Vlad Evanoff, in his book *Spin Fishing* says, "Since 1946 when spinning was first introduced into the USA ... there has been a tremendous growth in the popularity of this method. With this growth there has been a great improvement in the design of rods, reels, lures and lines ... used in both fresh- and salt-water spinning." Because of this more receptive approach the American market produces an extremely wide range of lures from many manufacturers.

A recent publication in *California Fish and Game* demonstrates the difference in attitudes. A survey of anglers was carried out on the Klamath river, which is more than twice the length of any British river. The main fishery is for steelhead trout, which are the sea-run form of our familiar rainbow, and also for king salmon (*chinook salmon*). The spring run of king salmon is in March–June and because of the high, dirty water they are rarely fished for at that time, most of the angling being carried out in July–November. The fish caught range from ½-pound immature steelhead to massive "submarine-sized" 60-pound kings. It is interesting that the average age of the anglers surveyed was 49 years; they were not young radicals or extremists. Surprisingly, the majority expressed little interest in taking the fish as food, though they were spending (on average) over 100 dollars on each trip. Even in the absence of restrictions on methods 72% *chose to spin*, 23% to use fly tackle and a mere 5% to use other (bait fishing) methods.

Is spinning too easy?

Without wishing to labour these differences in attitudes it is important to establish that spinning is NOT, in any way, less interesting, less skilful or less satisfying than fly, float, leger, free-line or indeed any other method. Surely in these days of enlightenment no one believes that spinning (or any other technique for that matter) is "too easy". A cursory discussion with other anglers will soon reveal that most of those who have "given spinning a try" have caught little or nothing during their first ventures. The one quality which seems to be necessary for success in this area of our sport – CONFIDENCE – is difficult to acquire. In the following pages, if we succeed in our aim, we will point the way to catching that vital first fish and subsequently to opening up the prospect of exploring an almost virgin field of fishing. It would be too much to hope that we may dispel any of the prejudice built over centuries against the methods which we use, but to those who exclaim, "I only fish with (fly, maggot, float, leger etc.)" our reply is "You don't know what you are missing. Even worse, you may never even realise the presence of the large fish you are not catching."

CHAPTER THREE

TACTICS OF THE HUNGRY FISH

Fish tactics

Most fish take the angler's lure because they are trying to eat it. Feelings of jealousy, frustration or annoyance, in the sense that we know them, are not involved, whatever you may have read to the contrary. The few exceptions to the feeding response involve defence of territories or competition for spawning areas and will be dealt with in other chapters.

The feeding behaviour of a fish is complicated, but depends mainly on its degree of hunger, and hunger is governed by its fullness. This, in turn, is affected by how much and how recently it has eaten. The more hungry the hunter then the more actively it will search for prey, the more persistently it will press home its attacks and the longer it will sustain its feeding spells.

Additional to the basic need for a meal are factors like water temperature, time of day and availability of prey. Generally, at higher water temperatures fish are more active, use more energy and eat more food. This means that, in most cases, the warmer the water the more energetically the fish will search for food and the more positively they are likely to bite. This temperature effect is relative and what is "warm" to a northern fish like the cod, salmon or pike, may be distinctly cold to a southern fish like the bass.

Certain fish may specialise in feeding at a particular time of day and, if we are to make the most of these feeding times, we must know when they are likely to occur. For example, if a fish feeds only in the daylight hours it will probably be most

16

likely to feed most voraciously at dawn, after a night of fasting. At times the presence of abundant prey may induce a frenzy of feeding, the most conspicuous example being the seething, slashing attacks of predators on surface-swimming schools of smaller fish.

Methods of attack
Predatory fish use four main strategies to catch their prey. Each strategy calls for a different approach from the angler.

1 Luring
Angler fishes and some other species use moving lures of their own to tempt smaller fish within range of their mouths. Lure fishermen could do worse than watch the style of an angler fish in an aquarium. Lying perfectly still on the "sea bed" it relies on perfect camouflage of form and colour to conceal it. The small, rather drab-coloured flag-like lure suspended on the fine filament over its head is extended and twitched seductively above the narrow thorny, crevice which represents the mouth. A poor-cod searching the sea bed for small but active beach fleas approaches the gently jigging lure. The angler fish (unlike its human counterpart) never shows signs of panic or haste and simply sustains the unhurried "swimming" movements of its bait. The smaller fish closes on the "artificial" and in a blur of snapping jaws it is engulfed and swallowed.

Other than the occasional angler fish caught by accident there seems to be no common method which is effective for such predators. Only a live bait, fished close to the sea bed on a slow retrieve, would seem to give any hope of success. However, the major difficulty in angling for luring predators is getting the bait to the right position for the fish to take it.

2 Ambushing
Predators which hunt from ambush are only a little less extreme than those just described and they present the angler with almost as many, though different, problems. Since the fish will not usually move far in its search for prey the lure must be placed virtually on the end of its snout. Some form of

camouflage is an important feature of fish hunting in this way and concealment may involve merging into the background by adopting coloration appropriate to the habitat. Consider how the pike, in its green and yellow livery, copies to perfection the dappled light that penetrates surrounding weeds; how the turbot alters the intensity of the gritty dorsal speckling and flips its fringing fins to hide its outline under the disturbed sediment. Perhaps the most subtle ambush of all is that of the john dory. With ragged trailing fins like fronds of drifting weed and a compressed, disc-like body it swims lethargically, leaning over to one side and looking nothing like a potential predator.

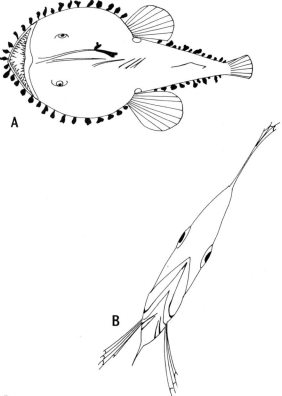

Figure 1
A Angler fish: a predator which uses a lure to attract prey. **B** John Dory: an "ambushing" fish which does not look at all like a potential predator.

All these fish have the common feature of a massive, capacious mouth to ensure that their strike, made possibly after a long wait, has a strong chance of being successful. The method of preparing for an attack is rather slow and is clearly seen in the pike. The fish carefully lines itself up on its victim before darting forward at high speed for the kill. Ambushers may, if necessary, stalk very slowly after particularly elusive prey and strike repeatedly at them.

3 Stalking

There are also strong similarities between fish which ambush their prey and those which stalk. The stalker sneaks forward to within striking distance before making the crucial lunge.

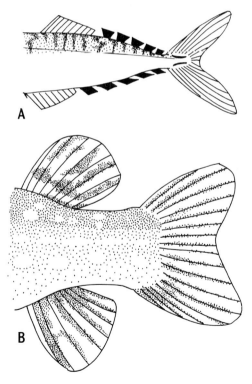

Figure 2
A Mackerel: a specialist "chaser" with a narrow tail wrist. **B** Pike: a specialist "accelerator" with a large fin area at the tail end.

Many predators will stalk single, lone, prey fish and the tactics which they use are often similar. The large fish fixes its eyes on the victim and turns slowly towards it, presenting the least fish-like profile of the body. Slowly it approaches, sculling gently with the paired fins or rippling the dorsal and ventral fins and often rolling the body to one side and thus looking even less like a predator. The tail is curved round to one side, thus setting the spring which provides the impetus for the final mighty burst of acceleration.

Stalking (and ambushing) predators will normally only take lures which are either fished *very* slowly, giving the fish time to line up and track them, or they may take baits which are presented at very close range. In using artificials for these fish it is usually worth several casts in each place to attract their attention and then to offer them a good opportunity to take.

4 Chasing

Hunters and chasers are the real meat and drink of the keen spin-fisher. Fish using this method generally chase, overtake, capture and swallow individual prey animals. They are mostly fast, slick swimmers with the form and ability to turn quickly. They catch their prey because it is less fleet of fin than they are or because they have the speed and stamina to herd, trap or exhaust it.

Examples of free-swimming chasers are mackerel, horse mackerel, sea trout and salmon, which cruise at high speeds in open water. Although they are fast swimmers these fish have rather poor acceleration, a design problem caused by specialisation to reduce drag (cut away tail-wrists and reduced fin areas). Because of this poor acceleration the mackerel, for example, catches only about 10-15% of the fish which it attacks, whereas a specialist accelerator like the pike may be successful in 80–90% of its attacks. Chasers compensate for this inefficiency by continual action, which brings them into contact with many prey, whereas fish which normally stalk or ambush their prey encounter only those victims which swim within their territory.

A second group of chasers includes near-bottom-living

species like cod or perch, which harry their prey from one hiding place to another. Lastly there are the more versatile opportunists like bass, trout, pollack and many others which can adapt their methods to the nature of the available food.

It will already be clear that there are no hard-and-fast differences between these four main strategies. Some fish are specialists and others are less fixed in their ways. There are also large numbers of fish which, although they normally feed on plants, insects or other small creatures will, at times, take larger and more active prey. This may occur only at certain seasons of the year or when the fish reach a large size, and is of special interest to the angler because it provides him with the opportunity of catching *speciment sized* members of such unlikely species as wrasse, mullet, roach, barbel and bream.

CHAPTER FOUR

MATCHING METHODS TO CONDITIONS

Choosing your lure

Whatever type of fish we wish to catch the best tackles, methods and lures depend on the same factors. Most important are the characteristics of the "prey" which the fish are seeking, such as shape, size, colour and type of movement. Also of importance is the way in which the angler's quarry is expected to take its prey. Each species has a different style but the usual ones involve a grab across the body from below, a similar attack from the flank, engulfing the victim from behind, or simply chopping or plucking at the tail end. Because of these differences the type of lure and the disposition of the hooks may be critical to success.

The depth at which the fish are swimming or feeding has a considerable influence on the angler's approach. Similarly the speed of water currents relative to the movement of the lure affects the suitability of a method. The nature of the "ground" over which the lures are to be fished must also be taken into account. For example, weed (soft snags), rocks, kelp stems, roots or branches (tough snags), sand, mud or gravel (clean and snag-free) will each require a different approach. The presence or absence of suspended matter in the water, which may take the form of turbidity (colour) or of lure-tangling fragments of algae, weed, eel-grasses and so on, can affect the method of fishing.

In some game fishing circles a tradition of matching the size of the bait to the temperature of the water has become almost a law. The basis for this theory is doubtful and, although the feeding activity of all fish is governed by water

22

temperature, it may well be that factors which are only indirectly due to temperature changes are responsible.

When we have considered the quirks of the fish we are after and the conditions in which we expect to find them, what next? Is there any way in which we might be able to attract them to the spot where we are fishing? Many predatory fish (and an even greater number of anglers) spend a lot of time simply searching the water for prey. What sort of signals inform the predators how to direct their searches? If we know this it might be possible to attract them to an area – almost in the way that coarse fishermen use ground bait or loose feed. In fast-moving active predators the sense of smell is usually of minor importance, but not so their reactions to vibrations and visual stimuli.

Good vibrations
The importance of vibration in attracting chasing predatory fish has been tested, mostly with active hunting-sharks. Pacific lemon sharks are attracted to low frequency sounds and move towards sources with frequencies of 20 to 50 cycles per second. Frequencies outside this range are *not* attractive to the fish. Another species, the grey shark, behaves in a similar way and underwater loudspeakers were used to attract them to intermittent bursts of low frequency sound. The sharks were also attracted to recordings of *fish struggling on a hook* or to those of a fish gripped in the jaws of a shark. It was concluded that the source of attraction was the "intense muscle sounds of the struggling fish". In another study "silky" sharks were attracted to "white noise" sounds between 25 and 1000 cycles per second, so proving that different species respond to different types of vibration.

It is certain that predatory fish, other than sharks, also search for the source of sounds and vibrations which signal food, yet most anglers continue to ignore this feature of attraction. Generally speaking, any species which feeds on large and active prey is, at least potentially, susceptible to attraction from a distance.

The foods of these predators fall into rather few groups which include fish, squid, crustaceans and large insects. The fish which they eat swim either by long-wave wriggling as in eels, short-wave sculling with the tail as in mackerel or by various forms of paddling with the fins. Squids and cuttle-fishes also propel themselves by undulations of fins but more often by pulsed jets of water from the siphon. Some large dragonfly larvae also use jet propulsion. Crustaceans such as crayfish, lobsters and squat lobsters, dart backwards pro-pelled by swift thrusts of the powerful, paddle-like tail. All these animals are characterised by their more or less stream-lined shapes and relatively swift movements. In choosing lures the shape and swimming action of the prey they are meant to represent should *always* be the prime consideration.

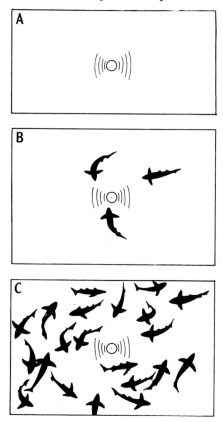

Figure 3
Low frequency sound from a hydrophone attracts many reef sharks within two minutes. **A** o minutes. **B** 30 seconds. **C** 2 minutes.

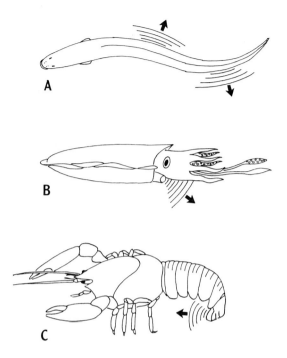

Figure 4
Types of swimming movement of prey animals. **A** Long wave
wriggling of the eel. **B** Pulsed jet propulsion of the cuttlefish. **C** Tail
flip escape reaction of the crayfish.

Flashers and teasers

If we return to the subject of how predatory fish *locate* their
prey we find that anglers have, in fact, devised several methods of using long-range signals as attractors. Usually these
attractors involve vibration or flash or both. Richard Walker
recalls that Col. Tattersall, fishing with live baits for pike,
used to repeatedly cast out and retrieve a large spoon with the
idea of tempting pike to the location of his live bait. Glass jars
containing live minnows were used in the past to attract
predatory fish, particularly perch, to the fishing position.
Anyone who has caught minnows in a trap will have noticed
the immediate increase in "customers" after the first minnow
enters and begins to twist, turn and flash in its efforts to
escape. There is nothing more effective than a keep-net full of
fish to attract pike or perch into the swim.

In sea fishing baited spoons, originally developed to attract flounders, have been extended in the form of flashers, rautos, baited-pirks and so on. To attract sharks in tropical waters it is common practice to beat the surface of the water with the paddle of the canoe or to shake halved coconut shells beneath the surface. Commercial tuna fishermen not only take great pains to "ground bait" with small live or dead fish but actually play powerful hoses onto the surface of the water to attract and *stimulate feeding* in the tuna. On a smaller scale, we are always pleased to see small fish leaping from the water at the approach of our spinning lure; for we know that this sort of bait-fish activity is likely to attract predators and may stimulate them to feed.

Anglers trolling for bill-fish, such as sailfish or marlin, in tropical waters, often fish a number of "teasers" to supplement the actual trolled baits. Presumably the idea is to keep the baited hooks in good condition as well as to attract fish from a distance and stimulate them to feed.

The most striking example of an attractor which works by flash and vibration is a device which brings the fish from a wide area but is *totally unsuitable* for inducing an attack (bite or strike). Off the Pacific coast of North America there are six species of salmon. Like our own Atlantic salmon they spawn in the fast-flowing streams and rivers of freshwater along the Pacific seaboard. They migrate to the sea to feed on the prolific shoals of small fish, planktonic-shrimps and squid off the shores of British Columbia and California.

All the Pacific salmon are swift-cruising, free-swimming hunters. They are fast-growing, streamlined and fiercely predatory. Some of the species stay close in shore and there feed actively, particularly in the salt water near the estuaries of rivers. Although these salmon will take lures during their upstream spawning migration, most of them do so with even less enthusiasm than the Atlantic salmon. In the sea however, as one might expect, they will take a wide variety of natural baits and imitations.

Despite the general view of the North American anglers being gimmicky and their lures as being too fanciful and "designed to catch the anglers rather than the fish", many of the methods employed are totally practical and based on sound principles. Fish strips mounted on the simplest of spinning flights; whole, small fishes similarly mounted; spinners and bucktail-flies, are all used to good effect for catching salmon.

Fishing is from the shore or from small boats and careful consideration is given to the fact that the different species feed at different depths. Notably, the small coho or blackmouth normally feeds very close to the surface and provides prime sport for anglers using light spinning tackle or powerful wet-fly gear with large bucktails. The larger chinook or king salmon is a deep-water feeder and lures must be presented at considerable depths. So that this can be achieved with light gear, a downrigger system is used.

To come to the original point, one of the best methods employed for catching chinook salmon is almost unbelievable to a British angler. It involves the ultimate attractor: a huge metal plate or flasher. So what is unusual? The salmon flasher is a sort of giant spoon (15 inches long and 6 inches wide), it has a split-ring and swivel at one end and travels in great swinging circles or loops on the end of the line. The diameter of the swing, if the angler gets it right, is about a yard. Tied to the tail end of the flasher is a nylon trace, and on the end of the trace is fixed a small silicone-rubber squid. The squids are what we have come to call wonder-shines or muppets. The Canadians have been using this type of squid for many years and refer to them as "hoochies". The range of colours and finishes available puts British manufacturers to shame.

The most interesting aspect of the method is that the trace between the huge flasher and the small lure may be as short as one foot and the wild gyrations of the metal spoon are intended, not just to attract the salmon, but to make the hoochy dart and twist wildly in its wake – *yet the fish still take it!* Would anyone here dream of trying a method like this? We doubt it, yet bass, cod, ling or pollack might be expected to respond to similar tactics. Scaled down, it could be applied to many other species.

Presumably the salmon assume that they have located other feeding salmon when they feel or see the movement of the flasher. The massive turbulence which it causes must be similar to that caused by the twists and turns of a feeding fish, and the jerking rubber squid simply looks like a small food animal (fish, squid or shrimp) swept out of control by the flourish of a mighty predator's tail.

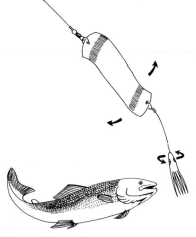

Figure 5
Large "Flasher" or "Dodger" used to attract predatory fish to a trolled lure.

There are, of course, simpler methods of simulating a feeding fish to attract others to the lure or bait. For example, there is no better way of attracting flounders than a fish already hooked, and the same is true of a mackerel hooked on a string of feathers. Since there are not many instances of "multi-hooked" spinning rigs, examples of fish-to-fish attraction are few, but commercial bass anglers fishing from boats off the south coast are known to fish two rods. When a fish is hooked on one bait it is left in position, twisting and turning until it attracts a second bass to the other bait. A well designed flasher rig would surely increase catches. Similar hookless spoons or attractors might be expected to work for perch and zander.

It must be obvious that attractors are less likely to be effective for ambushing or stalking predators, which are often solitary in their habits and do not normally swim far to obtain their food. With this proviso we suggest that any angler intending to spin for predatory fish should, when planning his campaign, consider the possible merits of long distance attraction and short range stimulation.

CHAPTER FIVE

THE PREDATOR

The dinner gong

Predatory fish can be considered to hunt in a series of stages. Firstly they must locate their prey and we have dealt with this at some length. Having located them they must then *recognise* them.

How does a predator recognise that something is food? Size must be the most important consideration but there are several other aspects to take into account. Sometimes, when a fish is landed, it is obvious what it has been eating. As the hooks were removed from the predator's jaws we have seen the mouths of bass and pollack teeming with sand eels, some of them still alive. We have landed pike with the tails of roach or dace protruding from the throat, and trout have coughed up minnows and bullheads as they bounced about on the grassy bank of the river. In cases like these it is easy to decide on the preferred size of prey, but they are the exceptions. Usually it is necessary to base judgments on what is known of the habits of our quarry.

It would be impossible to deal with every species of fish, even if the information was available, but are there any general rules? First, consider the size of the predator and the gape of its open mouth. Small species like perch, trout and mackerel, will generally feed on smaller animals than those eaten by, for example, pike or cod. As a rule the larger specimens of any species will eat larger prey (and take correspondingly large lures). For maximum sport a lure well within the size range of the prey being eaten will be best. A

29

larger lure will generally induce fewer bites; on the other hand it may give a better chance of really large fish. Sometimes an exceptionally large or small lure will produce a bite or two from fish which are already stuffed with food.

Big lures for big fish

Perhaps one of the most striking examples of the big bait/big fish relationship was encountered by Harry when he was on secondment for a year to the United Nations in Zambia, Africa. His job was to set up a laboratory for the study of lake and river chemistry. Because the outward journey was encumbered with the entire family's luggage most of the fishing tackle had to stay at home, but he found room for a light beach caster, a fixed spool reel and a few "spinners".

The first revelation came when Harry visited the local tackle shop in Lusaka. Most of the tackle on sale was of American origin. The so-called "spinning rods" were practically all short, whippy, wands totally foreign to his experience. He picked up and flexed every one until, at last, he found one with a stiffish action. On asking the price he was told that he could "have it cheap, because it was quite unsuitable for spinning". Money exchanged hands and Harry became the possessor of a rod which he subsequently used on waters all over Zambia. It has since become his favourite light boat rod with which he has now caught many of the larger sea fish species present in British waters.

The lures on sale in the Lusaka tackle shop were mostly familiar plugs and spoons from the USA but some of the most exciting items were the evocatively named "Zambesi spinners"; huge spoons 4 inches to 6 inches long, each with a single, long-shanked, wide-gaped hook. They resembled massive fly-spoons (the hook being brazed to a swivel on the concave side of the spoon) and were coloured in various combinations of red, copper and silver. Harry was informed that expert "tiger fishermen" often altered the casting properties and the action of the spinners by the addition of solder to the inner face of the spoon. Even more impressive were the enormous plugs, most of them larger than the average British chub or trout. "What are they for?" he whispered, feeling rather foolish. "Nile perch," came the reply. He selected a couple of hefty specimens, weighed them in his hand and felt thankful that he had brought the beach caster with him.

What fine teeth you have!

At every opportunity after making these purchases Harry was wielding his tackle on the shores of a lake or a river. His prime target was the fabulous tiger fish, deep bodied and brassy scaled, with a series of dark lines running along each flank. The most striking features of this fish are the incredibly long and sharply-pointed teeth which ornament the powerfully muscled and bony jaws. The purpose to which this dental equipment is put is that of disabling large prey-fish by chopping off fins or removing chunks of flesh. Because of this method of attack, lures *must* be protected by several inches of wire trace if chewed and broken line is to be avoided. Bright flashy swivels or clips, joining the trace to the main line, are definitely not recommended. The tiger fish will attack the links and in doing so will chomp through the nylon.

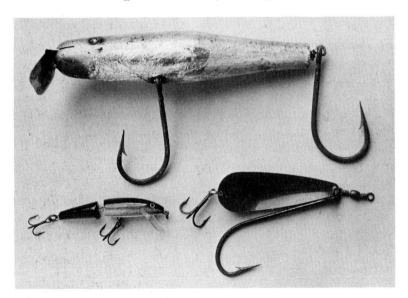

Large wooden plug and "Zambezi" spinner compared with a J.9. Rapala, showing the size of lure used to catch tiger fish.

Artificials were taken fiercely by the "tigers" but, because of the bony nature of the fishes' mouths, it was difficult to set the hook. This problem was magnified by the fantastic vitality of the fish which often came adrift as they hurled themselves into the air after the strike. After his first success, from the shore of Lake Kariba, Harry returned with a 7-pound fish taken on a 6-inch spoon. His pride was somewhat deflated when he was informed by a South African colleague that it was "hardly worth keeping". The record for the lake was 39 pounds – a real dream (or nightmare) of a fish.

Despite having fished Lake Kariba (175 miles long, 50 miles wide and 370 feet deep) Harry was still totally unprepared for the immensity of Lake Tanganyika. This was brought home to him during a sampling trip, by boat, with an Irish colleague. In the heat of the day they allowed the boat to drift for a while so that they could cool down with a swim. Harry was quite calm and relaxed until he was told that there were 4800 feet of water beneath him. The thought was overwhelming and he clambered back into the boat, never to swim in that part of the lake again.

To return to the fishing. From the boat the little spinning rod and fixed spool reel proved to be ideal for catching yellow-fish (a type of barbel) of 2–3 pounds and, by using Toby spoons, numerous Nile perch of up to about 12 pounds were also landed. However, Harry never was content with anything but the biggest and out came the good old beach caster and the monster plugs. He cast them from the shores and trolled them along behind the boats but the results were modest, with catches topped by a 16-pound Nile perch (almost in the "fry" class) and a 12-pound tiger fish. Aware of the fish which he was *not* catching Harry decided that the plugs were just not big enough and resorted to legering with a live 3-pound yellow fish. All his efforts were to no avail but it was soon clear that the idea was right when a visitor came back with a 70-pound Nile perch. "How did you get that one?" enquired Harry. "I was playing a yellow-fish when it was taken by the perch," he said.

Harry was speechless, and only those of us who know Harry can appreciate the depth of his emotion.

Apart from this emphasis on big baits for big fish there were other lessons to be learned on Lake Tanganyika. Harry put in a good deal of effort spinning, from a small boat, for the elusive Nile perch. On one occasion he was thrilled to find the sort of activity which "shouts out" *fish!* A huge shoal of sardine-like kapenta were under assault by larger predators. Over a wide area the little silver fish were spraying from the water and the heads, tails and fins of their aggressors were breaking the surface everywhere. The boat was drifted through the area of activity and a Toby, of appropriate size, was cast out and retrieved repeatedly without so much as a sniff. At the other side of the shoal, after a 600 yard drift, Harry changed the lure, motored back up (well clear of the fish) and began a second drift. Once again the lack of action was impressive. For a third time the drift was repeated, this time with a white, red-headed plug, but with no greater effect. Still the predators were feeding in a frenzied fashion all around the boat. It was almost unbelievable. Quite suddenly the shoals dispersed and Harry was left to contemplate his failure. What had he done wrong? Why did the fish ignore his lure? The size and action of the spoon lures had been as near to the prey fish as seemed possible and they must have been *seen* by countless predators.

He asked a fishery biologist how many kapenta would be in a school of the size which he had seen and was told that "It could have been as many as half a million, depending on the depth to which they were swimming." It seemed to Harry that his failure may have been due to the old, old reason; the availability of too much natural food. The chance of a predator selecting his lure from the host of sardines was probably quite small – a masterly understatement!

On the next occasion that he saw a similar phenomenon it was on a much smaller scale. This time he was more patient and watched the pattern of movement shown by the rolling predators. They were mostly active near the surface around the edges of the "sardine" school. This time the Toby was cast only to the margins of the area of activity and he had fine sport with Nile perch of up to 12–13 pounds. An object lesson in the reason for (defensive) schooling by small prey fish.

Shoaling for safety

Many small "forage" fish form schools for purposes of defence. All the fish in a school will accelerate, wheel, turn and slow down almost as one, with never a bump nor jostle. Just like a flight of birds, they are able to perform these high-speed manoeuvres by reacting to the movements of their nearest neighbours which they can see and feel (through the lateral line sense). Fish gathered into tight groups are less conspicuous to predators than are lots of scattered individuals. Also, many pairs of eyes may (just about) be better than one when it comes to detecting the approach of a killer. A hunter which needs to track and line up its prey could well have problems selecting a target from the bobbing, weaving school and a chasing predator might easily be distracted into a series of tiring chases involving one fish after another, each new chase giving the other potential victims a "breather".

It has been shown *conclusively* that predators, both in freshwaters and in the sea, will soon pick out members of a school which:

1 look slightly different;

2 behave erratically;

3 become *separated* from the main group of fish.

In the light of these facts Harry's experiences are easy to explain.

One or two other aspects of the kapenta/Nile perch story are of interest. The commercial fisherman of Lake Tanganyika, in answer to Harry's queries, said that the kapenta spent most of the hours of daylight at depths of up to 200 feet. At night they migrated up to the surface. Presumably the fish which Harry had seen were driven up by an attack from below. Of the three species of Nile perch present in the lake Harry had, of course, been catching the smallest. The largest type, which attains 200 pounds, may be caught at depths of over 600 feet. At this weight it might be said that the danger lay in the fish catching Harry!

Before any of this information could be acted on it was the end of the year and Harry and his family returned home. However, many of his observations on huge tropical lakes and rivers have their parallels in and around Britain.

Keeping in shape

Our own pike has received more than its fair share of study. Pike feed selectively, that is to say they have been shown to *prefer* certain sizes and species of fish as food. Young pike, of about 10 inches in length, prefer prey of about $1\frac{1}{2}$ inches long. Fish of 18 inches have a preferred prey size of $2\frac{1}{2}$ inches, while larger pike will choose correspondingly large victims. Another very important aspect of size is that big baits can be located at greater distances than small ones. So, all things being equal, a big bait is more likely to attract the attentions of a predator than a small one.

Size of prey is only one feature among many. The next thing for the lure fisherman to take into account is the *shape*

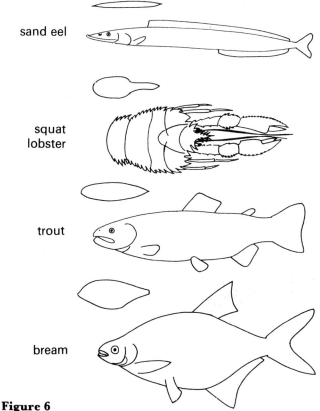

sand eel

squat
lobster

trout

bream

Figure 6
For efficient foraging the predator acquires a search image of the shape of its prey.

of the common food items. Are they thin or fat, slimline or deep-bodied? There is probably not much point in looking for an exact imitation and, as long as your lure is roughly the right shape, most predators do not seem to be particularly fussy. Pike which are used to feeding on, for example, bream, will be on the look-out for fish about three times as long as they are deep. Bass which are searching along wrack-covered ledges for wrasse are also likely to be "switched on" by a meaty mouthful. In contrast, sea trout, pollack or mackerel with sand eels on their mind will have a fixation for fish about eight times as long as they are deep. The ideal lure should be chosen accordingly. Prawns and squids will create a roughly conical or wedge-shaped search image. Crayfish or squat lobsters may produce an over-riding impression of trailing pincers or dangling legs. If trout fly anglers have shown it to be worthwhile to make each tiny imitation closely represent a certain insect, then it *must* be even more important to match the form of a decent square meal.

Movement

Taking another leaf out of the fly angler's book, *movement* is a key factor in recognition. Fish detect the movements of their chosen prey in two ways – by vision and by sensing vibrations (waves) through the lateral line system. The brain of the predator analyses this information and decides whether the swimming speed, flicker rate and throb signal say food? – appropriate food? – vulnerable food? If all three answers are acceptable the fish will go into attack mode.

Movements (like size and shape) are generally characteristic of each type of prey. For example, some bait animals will swim quickly and others slowly. Small fish will generally flicker or vibrate at high frequencies (say several times per second); larger specimens will wriggle along at a slower pulsing rate. Small fry and sprats seem to twinkle through the water while eels and lampreys move with sedate undulations. The key words with most healthy swimming animals are *regular rhythm*. Predators respond quickly to any slight deviation from the normal and prey creatures which have lost their rhythmic swimming pattern are often as good as dead.

The value of colour

Colour in fish has several important functions, the most familiar one being camouflage, which is generally achieved in one of two ways. The many silver-sided, counter-shaded fish – sprats, sand eels, roach, dace, sea trout, salmon and so on – are trying to "disappear" by reflecting their surroundings. (Think of the illusion created by the mirror at the back of a supermarket display if you want to get the idea.) Also, by reflecting every scrap of light, they merge into even a well-lit background.

A second form of camouflage is simply that of matching and merging into the surroundings. Flat fish are particularly good at this but most bottom-living or weed-haunting species do the same.

The "give away" for the silver camouflage is usually flash or eyes (which they are unable to silver effectively). For the bottom-living forms, mismatching of colours and patterns is the problem. This results from either being the correct colour on the wrong background or *vice versa*. If colour was not so important in concealment then fish, cuttlefish and other potential prey would not have developed such fancy colour change abilities.

The keen lure fisherman should always bear in mind that not all colours are likely to be attractive to predators. Just as wasps have black and yellow bands and distasteful butterflies often have bright bold colour patterns, so there are warning colours underwater. Very strongly-coloured, conspicuous lures may actually frighten predators and there are examples of black fins in poisonous fish like weevers; large, black-eye spots in cuttlefish, etc. and bold stripes, spots and colour patterns in certain wrasses which may well be KEEP-OFF signs.

The easy option

Most predatory fish will go for the easiest option. For example, pike have been shown to eat those fish which are most abundant and therefore easiest to come by. In Lake Michigan the pike switched from smelts to shad as their preferred prey when the latter migrated inshore to spawn in May-August. The significant thing is that the pike completely ignored the abundant perch (a species which they usually devour with relish) because they become preoccupied with either smelt or shad. The same sort of switching and pre-occupation has been shown to occur in zander and small-mouth bass.

Most of the studies on prey selection have been carried out with largemouth bass. These voracious, perch-like fish of the North American continent have pretty broad tastes. In a couple of private ponds near our homes in Dorset we used to catch quite a few (introduced) largemouth on a wide range of baits and lures. The fish would inspect any object in or on the water and quite often the float in use for tench or roach would be nosed with a view to consumption as food. After a close examination the bass usually melted away into the greeny-brown, clayey water but occasionally, if the float was twitch-ed, it would be taken with a gulp.

Despite their huge mouths these fish are, in fact, rather fussy and have definite preferences for particular types of prey fish. In one experiment it was shown that largemouths preferred 'dace' and newts to golden-shiners and right at the bottom of the list were domestic goldfish. The conclusion was that the bass chose their food on the basis of:

1 how easy it was to catch;
2 its taste (palatability);
3 the way in which it behaved;
4 its size.

So the general picture is clear; our lure must look and move like a "favourite prey". Its size, shape, speed and rhythmic swimming movements have to be of the right kind but the lure must signal its vulnerability:

1 by being separated from its fellows (shoal-mates);
2 by moving erratically, jerkily or slower than normal;
3 by travelling in an unusual direction; and
4 by standing out from the background (being slightly off-colour).

A few examples of the right food doing the wrong thing may help to suggest some ideas. A hunting predatory fish will expect to encounter its prey "heading for cover", cover being the weeds, rocks, pier piles, sandy sea or river-bed or the water surface. A lump of food (lure) heading in the opposite direction will be asking for trouble.

Many small fish and other creatures will do their utmost *not* to look like food. Mike has often seen small rudd hanging motionless, heads down, in the calm still water of lakes. This posture might well be suicidal if it were recognised by hunting pike, perch or zander, but presumably it is safer than swimming in normal fashion. Bass will often ignore a stiff, gently sinking prawn, only attacking when the crustacean flicks its tail-fan and tries to gain a hiding place. It seems that the rigid prawn either does not look like food or possibly seems to be a tricky mouthful, with its sharp, saw-toothed rostrum sticking out like a spear.

For out-and-out predators such as pike, erratic movements of prey fish are like a dinner gong. Takes can be induced by jerking a lure or fishing it sink-and-draw in front of a known or suspected lie. Many territorial fish, including salmon, will also respond to a plug, spoon or spinner twitched or dabbled on their nose. The repeated jerky movements may suggest the presence of a school of prey fish. This may stimulate feeding or simply catch the predator's attention, allowing it to anticipate the chance of a successful strike.

You can't fool a skipjack

The importance of this "ground bait" effect produced by the presence of schools of forage fish is well known to some commercial fishermen. In the Hawaiian tuna fishery the fast-swimming skipjack tuna are caught on hook, rod and fixed lines. Live fish are used to bait the hooks and the fishermen go to great pains to catch small sea fish (nehu) for bait. The fish are kept alive in specially constructed live bait wells within the fishing boats.

Just like any other "anglers" quite often, when they need bait most, it is hardest to come by (remember that pike session when the dace refused to bite, or the turbot fishing charter trip when the mackerel would not cooperate?). To make up for this problem an attempt was made to breed and supply tuna bait in large quantities at a low price, the most convenient fish to farm for bait being the African *Tilapia*. These were reared in freshwater ponds and sold to the tuna fishermen.

As mentioned earlier, to attract the tuna and to stimulate them into a feeding frenzy the fishermen do two things. First, they play hoses on the surface of the sea to simulate the activity of many small fish. Second, the little live baits are scattered into the sea by the shovelful. The hooks with their live baits are then plonked in the midst of the frantic tuna. Despite their strange appearance, for the *Tilapia* resemble wrasse more than the herring-like nehu which are the skipjack's natural food, they were reasonably effective baits and the tunny took them quite well *but not as well as the natural food fish*. The conclusions were:

1 slightly more schools of tuna were attracted by "feeding" with natural bait than with *Tilapia*;
2 nehu (natural baits) produced more fish per minute than *Tilapia*; and
3 large skipjack tuna were more fussy (selective) than small ones.

The complete picture

To sum up, it *does* matter which bait or lure you use to attract and tempt a predator and by simulating frenzied activity of small bait fish it is possible not only to attract predatory fish to the scene but also to get them feeding.

Fish which specialise in particular prey – for example, sand eel, brit, minnows and so on – will almost always need to be tempted with a more or less accurate imitation of their normal food. Generalist feeders, like pike, bass or trout will only require this approach when some particularly juicy item is exceptionally abundant.

Apart from these basics there are no hard and fast rules about lure selection. However, the following important details should be considered – probably in this order – when choosing a lure.

Try to represent the natural prey *at the time and place of fishing*. Size, shape, movement, position in the water and, if possible, colour and recognition patterns are important. If it is possible to achieve all of these characteristics it will be a miracle, but even a reasonable approximation should catch fish. This is, of course, assuming that there are predatory fish in the area; that the predators are feeding or can be induced to feed; and that the lure is not totally lost in a profusion of natural prey. In the latter case, having tried to match the chosen food and failed, it can be profitable to use a lure which is conspicuously different from the prey. If this also fails then stop spinning, make every effort to get hold of some natural baits and fish with these – always a good bet. We have spent many frustrating hours trying to catch minnows, sand eels, etc. when our quarry was mad-on but preoccupied.

CHAPTER SIX

TOOLS OF THE TRADE

Choosing tackle

How should you go about buying spinning tackle? It is possible to offer advice but in the end it will depend on

1. what is available;
2. how much you propose to spend;
3. how much effort you are prepared to put into making your own gear; and
4. personal choice.

Because of mail-order the availability of standard items is now much wider than it was a few years ago. However, if you consider buying by mail-order you must give the matter plenty of thought, for it may not be possible to examine the equipment before ordering it. To some extent you "get what you pay for" but, when starting from scratch, most of the investment should go into the reel. No matter what sort of reel you buy, be it fixed spool or multiplier, quality counts. There *are* some good, reasonably priced reels available, but it takes experience to pick them and experience can be expensive. Perhaps the best guide is to scan photographs in magazine features and books and see what the "experts" are using. It is often heartening to see that the "experts", whether they are bottom- or spin-fishermen, often use equipment that is very similar.

Do-it-yourself generally involves rods and terminal tackle. Rod making can range from whipping the rings onto a blank to buying a kit, together with fittings, bits and pieces and making your own. Often it is difficult to produce your own rod cheaper than an off-the-shelf model (especially if you keep an eye out for sale bargains), but the advantages come in details of construction.

Personal choice of equipment can result in one angler using a 6-foot, crank-handle rod and a small multiplier whilst his (or her) pal fishes equally effectively with a 12-foot "carp" rod and fixed spool reel. There is literally no accounting for taste and, in the following pages, all we can do is point out the benefits or disadvantages of particular items of tackle.

We tend to use very similar types of rods and reels but the differences are perhaps more interesting than the similarities. Harry, being larger and more substantially built (his description of a fat body), tends to fish with a slightly heavier, more powerful, rod. Again, the positioning of the reels on the handles of our rods is totally different. There is no detectable difference in the casting, fishing or catching properties of the tackle in our own respective hands but neither of us feels completely happy with the other's tackle.

Rods

Our spinning rods are called upon to fish with a wide range of lure-weights and line-strengths. The test curves of the rods range from $1\frac{1}{4}$ to $2\frac{1}{2}$ pounds and will generally handle weights of $\frac{1}{4}$ ounce to $1\frac{1}{2}$ ounces without complaint. The line strengths used vary from 5–6 pounds up to 15–18 pounds breaking strain. Specialist rods may be obtained for use with extralight or heavy tackle, but it should be remembered that fishing with heavier rods can be very tiring and this is often critical in a long spinning session.

Hollow glass- or carbon-fibre rods, of the calibre suggested, are effective with most lures from small bar-spoons and plugs to 6-inch wobbling spoons and small pirks. They cast well and (most important) for us they have hooked, played and landed every type of fish from titchy 10-inch trout to ponderous 30-pound pike and salmon.

Every rod is a compromise in its design characteristics and it is possible to make rods which either cast, strike, or play the fish better than the average, but overall the compromise will be most useful.

How long should a spinning rod be? It does not matter much from the point of view of most fishing conditions but remember that while it is possible to fish close in with a long rod, either by standing a little further back or up or downstream, it is not possible to manoeuvre fish or lures around snags with a rod which is too short. Harry, before the start of the salmon season, has been known to spend hours walking the beat with clippers and bow-saw making certain that if there are any troublesome obstacles on the bank (very large bushes, overhanging branches, etc.) they are trimmed so he is able to squeeze past or manipulate his rod over the top. Other anglers have had hours of entertainment watching his efforts but Harry had the last laugh. Because of this preparation, over the years, he has caught several fish which he would otherwise probably have lost.

In general the longer the rod, the more satisfactory it will prove to be. Only rarely is a rod less than about 9 feet in length any advantage – possibly under trees or in confined spaces. But it is interesting to note that most accurate competition casting work is done with short rods (go to any game fair and see this); so presumably precise aim is one advantage of a short rod. In actual fishing conditions and situations this is probably of marginal value and we manage to fish easily in small overgrown streams with our 11-foot "poles".

On the subject of casting accuracy there is no substitute for continued practice when it comes to developing good technique. The most important skill to acquire is that of *judging the range*. There is nothing more frustrating than hooking the far bank when this is inaccessible. The outcome of this type of miscast can be a lost lure (expensive) and/or a frightened fish; the latter is often the most annoying aspect. To avoid the disastrous overcast into the far bank, or wrack-bed

1 watch the lure as it travels through the air;
2 slow down the latter stages of the cast by thumbing the spool (multiplier) or allowing the index finger to brush the line as it leaves the spool (fixed spool reel);
3 in desperation, stop the cast suddenly and, by following through with the rod tip, try to lessen the splash of the lure as it hits the water.

One of the minor problems with long rods is that of housing them in car boots or interiors. However, since few sections are more than 6 feet long they generally fit inside saloons of modest size but we did know one fisherwoman who, when changing cars, would reject any with a boot too small to accommodate her favourite rods.

Reels

There are perhaps more fallacies and misunderstandings about reels than any other aspect of fishing tackle. When we were first invited to go salmon fishing on the River Avon we took our normal spinning tackle, which included the trusty Cardinal fixed spool reels. On seeing our gear, one of the regular salmon anglers asked us, rather patronisingly, if we would like to borrow a multiplier. Harry immediately produced one from his tackle bag and replied that we did not normally use them for salmon spinning. "Why ever not?" he asked, and expressed surprise when we said we thought our fixed spool reels were just as effective. Also, if required, we could cast lighter lures with them more accurately. He clearly thought that we would not be able to control or land a big fish.

On this Avon fishery it is a custom for the anglers to change banks at 12 o'clock, so after a biteless morning we had to fish the stretch which the other salmon fisherman had been flogging all morning. We saw him shake his head as he watched us testing our tackle before setting off for the afternoon session. A quarter of an hour later he was shaking his head again (this time in disbelief) as Harry carried a 20-pound fresh-run salmon up to the fishing hut to be weighed.

What we are trying to emphasize is that the type of reel makes no difference to the line strength which is suitable for a particular type of fishing. If 4-pound line can be used to cast the tackle, cope with the snags, set the hook and stand the strain and stress in controlling the fish, then it is equally suitable on a centre pin reel, fixed spool, multiplier, sidecast or fly reel. The presence of a slipping clutch on geared reels (fixed spools or multipliers) is no substitute for skill, judgment and the use of appropriate finger or thumb pressure when playing a fish.

Slipping clutches (including star drags) must be used correctly at all times. The first thing we do after tackling up is to take the lure in one hand (avoiding the hooks) and pull so as to flex the rod over or near to its test curve, the clutch being set (by trial and error) so that it will *just give line*. The most critical instant is when a fish takes and has to be struck. If the tension is too light it will not set the hooks and, at worst, the spool will over-run, causing a tangle; if the tension is too great it will fail to give line on the strike and a breakage may result.

It is much easier to keep the spool moving than to get it started, so the clutch should always be set with this in mind. The elasticity of the rod and the stretch in nylon lines will cushion the major jerks and pulls, but it is up to you to judge when the line is in danger of breaking and to ease off the tension.

We have seen anglers screw the tension right down and try to haul fish in by brute strength. This may work with small fish or very heavy lines but if you get a decent fish on, it must inevitably result in a breakage. On one occasion we even saw a rod broken in this way.

Some very good anglers do not use the clutch on a geared reel. They prefer to "backwind", leaving the anti-reverse mechanism disengaged and allowing the spool and handle to rotate backwards. A set of gears has considerable frictional resistance and, if a fish runs hard, it may be necessary to actually wind the handle backwards. There is no obvious advantage to this method over the proper clutch control and the knack of backwinding has to be learned. Presumably there is always some risk of over-run when using this technique but, in the rare event of a clutch seizure or mechanical damage, it can be a very useful emergency tactic.

Each of the reels (and the matching rods) mentioned above was designed with a particular style of fishing in mind. For casting *extremely* light "baits", fly tackle is the only possibility. However, when it comes to slightly heavier lures, $\frac{1}{8}$-ounce upwards, the fixed-spool reel comes into its own. Since the fixed-spool reel is ideal for casting and handling weights of up to a couple of ounces, it serves for the majority of spinning situations; there is no real need to use any other reel except for reasons of personal choice. Multiplying reels are suitable for casting heavier weights of about $\frac{1}{2}$-ounce upwards, but the casting technique is slightly more demanding and in strong headwinds the multiplier can cause an inexperienced angler problems. Here are the points to look for when purchasing a fixed spool reel, or any reel for that matter.

1 The action must be smooth with no tendency for jerkiness when the handle is turned.
2 The bale arm should have a roller bearing for the line; the bale arm springs and trip mechanism must be positive and reliable.
3 The slipping clutch should be *smooth* and easily adjusted over a wide range of tensions. Turn the spool by hand at different settings on the range to check this.
4 The reel must have a *minimum* of knobs, lugs and projections to snag or tangle the line.
5 Several spare spools, loaded with different line strengths, increase the versatility of the tackle.
6 If sea fishing is to be the main use, avoid reels with lots of aluminium or mild steel on display.

Reels for use in sea fishing should be, as far as possible, "salt-water proof" although in practice none is totally impervious to salt corrosion. Most good quality reels can be used for spinning in the sea provided they are well washed afterwards.

It is no use having a good rod and reel if the line you are using is not suitable. A sharp strike from a stiff-action rod may snap a fine line even if the clutch setting is correct. Conversely, even with a soft action rod, a reel which is screwed up tight will result in breakage if a powerful fish lunges unexpectedly after it is hooked.

Lines

Line varies enormously in quality. Poor lines are useless for spinning, so try to avoid line that is glossy and springy – however attractive the price may be. But remember that bulk buying of line can greatly reduce the cost, so if you have a few pals who use similar strength lines, a 1000 m spool may be shared to good effect. If you have bought nylon line, keep it out of direct sunlight when not in use. Kevin Maddocks reviews different lines in his book *Carp Fever* and the criteria which he outlines apply to every sort of fishing. One note of caution. It is best to buy lines from a tackle shop with a large turnover. We know of a general store where lines in the fishing tackle area have been on the shelf for at least 6 years. Unlike the content of your hip-flask, lines do not improve with age!

Since much spinning is in open water, and fish are likely to have a good look at the line, it is worth using neutrally coloured or clear lines rather than those that are tinted and conspicuous. It has been conclusively shown that jigs fished on thick or coloured nylon monofilament catch less squid than those on finer, colourless line. The same must surely be true of most predatory fish.

Hooks

The last piece of equipment is the hook. After testing various shapes, sizes and strikes using a variety of tackle, we are satisfied that the most important factors are the sharpness of the hook, and the size of the barb. Even with 3-pound breaking strain line, on a very whippy float rod, medium sized (2 and 4) hooks could be "set" *providing they were very sharp* and the barb was not too large. Good quality hooks are very important; one of our friends lost a 30-pound salmon when the hook snapped as he was preparing to gaff it.

It is at this stage that most books on spinning would launch into an extensive catalogue of lures. However, spinning is just not that complex. The range of named lures produced by manufacturers is exhaustive, not to say exhausting, considering that all of them fall into only a few main types.

In the following chapters we shall try to explain how to choose the lure which is best suited to the conditions and most likely to interest fish you are trying to catch.

You may now be wondering why we have not given details of various spinning rigs. How long are our traces? How many swivels do we use? Which lures need an anti-kink device? The answer to these questions is that, usually, we only have a single link-swivel at the end of the main line. In those relatively few cases where other rigs are useful, these are described in the appropriate chapters.

CHAPTER SEVEN

PIKE

The pike's year

For once we were not fishing, but were pike-watching alongside a deep ditch that ran away from the main river. The ditch cut across the meadow as straight as the proverbial ruler; an old ditch with reeds and sedges crowding its edges, with here and there a young alder tree rooted in the soil at the side, its branches hanging down towards the water. We moved slowly along the bank, making certain that we could not be seen by any fish in the shallow water. Suddenly we both stopped dead; down below was what we had been hoping to see. There in the dim light were four log-like shapes, one much larger than the others. A big female pike well on the way to 30-pounds had entered from the river and, with her three lesser consorts, had made her way to a thick clump of reeds where, in an orgy of thrashing fins and turbulent "rust" flecks she shed almost four pounds of tiny translucent eggs, each one just over 1/16 inch in diameter. The spawning over, the pike left as quickly and silently as they had entered.

In the cold April water the little eggs, glued to the tough weed stems, would begin to develop. Many of the eggs would be infertile, becoming opaque and falling prey to the tiny aquatic fungi and bacteria which infest the ditch. Many more would be rasped and eaten by wandering snails, sucked by tiny spider-like mites or torn to pieces and swallowed by sticklebacks.

But in due course, like pieces of knotted thread, the tiny pikelings would emerge from their eggs and cling tightly to reed and weed stems, feeding on microscopic algae, ciliates, rotifers and water-fleas, all the time their numbers being reduced by continuous depredations of mantis-like water scorpions, shiny water-beetles with curved piercing fangs and the even stronger, crushing jaws of camouflaged caddis larvae.

The water would be warming up quickly now and the young pike growing rapidly. As they increased in size and became more like their parents in appearance, they would begin feeding on larvae and the fry of other fish which had hatched from eggs much later than themselves. In the river a few of the young pike would be eaten by trout and salmon parr, many would fall prey to marauding perch, but the majority would be snapped up by the arrow-like lunges of their elder brothers and sisters. At a year old the survivors (now weighing about four ounces) would be feeding on roach, dace and minnows – subsequently to be their food for the remainder of their lives. By the following year the male pike would weigh about a pound, the female about 1¼ pounds. Most of the pike of both sexes would by now be mature, with the larger fish developing first, and by the age of eight the female pike will be twice the weight of the males.

The above account is more or less typical of pike in a rich lowland river such as the Dorset Stour, or in some lakes. In many other waters growth is considerably slower. In waters where the annual temperatures are generally low, the pike, like other fish, grow more slowly but could ultimately reach a greater size than their counterparts which live at higher temperatures.

Mike's first pike

It was in such a lake in the North of England that Mike saw his first pike.

When he was in his early teens his summer holidays were usually spent fishing in the sea. Wrasse, coalfish, codling, flounder and plaice were his normal catches but it was on one such holiday that he discovered coarse fish. The discovery was made in a flooded, derelict limestone quarry on the coast of Northumberland. On the south side of the quarry rugged, grey-stone cliffs of hard carboniferous limestone fell almost sheer to the water surface, with only one or two access points to ledges near water level. Few plants gained a root-hold on the steep rock faces and the water was extremely deep and crystal clear. The north bank, 20 or 30 yards across the deep water, was a meadow of stony soil thinly clothed in short grass which sloped gently over a scree-like bed. Along the shallower slopes of the north margin dense thickets of feathery-leaved, red-stemmed water milfoil were interspersed with clumps of pond weed with oval, wax-coated, floating leaves.

During the first couple of summers Mike fished intensively, first for the small perch which were unbelievably abundant; then, as his skill increased, for roach which ranged in size from the usual 8–10 inches, up to a massive fish of $2\frac{1}{2}$ pounds caught, as dusk fell, on a margin-fished lump of bread. Eels were also present in this quarry and many of them were very large. Almost every evening Mike was down at the "pond" legering for them with herring-strip or lobworm and he landed some very big specimens, the largest being 4 feet long. It was whilst fishing for eels that he caught his first pike. He was slowly winding in his lobworm bait when there was a sharp jerk and on the end of his line was a superb little fish of about one pound; not only the first pike he had caught but also the first he had seen alive.

On the following day he took the bus into Alnwick to visit the tackle shop and buy some "pike spinners" and 10-pound nylon. He sought the advice of the shop assistant but, in this game fishing area, it turned out to be Hobson's choice. The "spinners" were simple, spoon-shaped spoons. They were in two sizes, $1\frac{1}{2}$ inches and 2 inches, chromium plated and armed with a single tail treble.

Lessons learned

In the following weeks a few pike up to 5–6 pounds in weight fell to the spoons. The tackle was quite unsuitable for spinning but, by improvising, it was possible to fish many of the better spots. The rod used was a 12-foot tank aerial purchased through the mail order columns of *Angling Times* and the reel a small wooden centrepin. Two basic methods were used. The first involved stripping off a few yards of line and swinging the spoon out between the weedbeds. For the second (to give a longer retrieve) the spoon was laid on a stone in the water's edge and thirty or forty yards of line were paid off as Mike walked away along the bank. The spoon was then reeled back parallel to the bank. Both tactics were successful and the excitement was intense because it was possible to see almost every "take".

Gradually, patterns emerged from these simple spinning activities. The $1\frac{1}{2}$-inch spoon took many more perch than pike, while the reverse was true of the larger spoon. Other lures were tried, without much thought involved in the choice. Metal devon minnows were tried and found wanting in the still, clear water; the retrieve needed to be much too fast to make them work effectively. Cheap plastic plugs (floaters) caught a few fish and often resulted in exciting surface strikes as they wriggled above the weedbeds.

Noting the success of the larger spoons Mike invested several weeks' pocket money in a "Jim Vincent Broads Spoon", a $5\frac{1}{2}$-inch plate of (apparently) stainless steel. The idea was to try and tempt one of the bigger pike, for he had seen one or two monsters following eel baits on the retrieve. His first attempts with the big spoon were not encouraging; it flapped and swung about in the water beautifully and it had plenty of weight to cast well out, even on his crude tackle, but

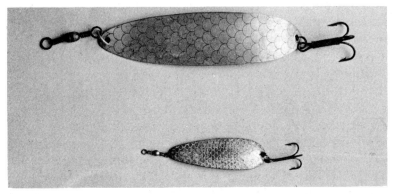

The "Jim Vincent" spoon (top) is a good pattern for big pike. Smaller spoons such as the $2\frac{1}{4}$ inch "Salar" are less likely to pick out the very large fish.

nothing showed any interest. Confidence soon ebbed and the "Jim Vincent" was consigned to the tackle bag to be dug out now and then for a few casts, more in hope than in expectation.

One day, at the end of August, Mike was working his way along the north bank casting across towards the steep cliffs and retrieving as deep and slow as he dared. Just as he reached the narrowest point he was staring intently into the black depths for a first glimpse of the twisting, flashing spoon. There it was! – gradually its form became clear as it "swam" up the steep-sloping shelf. Suddenly a huge green shape emerged from the darkness and swept in a graceful curve past the spoon, narrowly missing the stern treble. He was so startled that he whipped the lure from the water and held it dangling from the tip of the tank aerial as he attempted to control the trembling hand and pounding heart. Would it come again? He guessed not, thinking that the pike must have seen him standing there. Foolishly, as it turned out, he swung the lure out ten feet and began to draw it back simply by slowly raising the rod tip. A couple of seconds elapsed and suddenly there was the big fish again – but this time it clearly held the "Jim Vincent" firmly clamped in its massive jaws. Little of the spoon was visible, but the swivel stuck out from the left side of the fish's mouth and on the right the hook hung loosely. Again panic set in and Mike struck wildly, the rod creaked and bent, the pike's jaws parted – and the spoon twanged back and clattered onto the bank.

Despite ten minutes of further effort the fish did not reappear, but Mike had learned two valuable lessons. First, that the big spoon was capable of stimulating large pike to attack, and second, *never* to spin in a half-hearted fashion. Certainly, if he had cast out and retrieved from the reel, the spoon would have had more forward momentum and the rod would have been in a more appropriate position to enable a firm strike. The chances of setting the rather crude hooks would also have been improved.

Following these first attempts at pike spinning there was a long interval in which much time was devoted to reading about pike. It was clear to Mike that these were his sort of fish. Even the small ones were a fair size. At least one approach to their capture involved an active, energetic, searching tactic quite different from many of the sit-and-wait or chuck-and-chance-it methods with which he was already familiar. Also, pike spinning represented a real challenge and there was obviously plenty of room for improvement in lures and technique. So far the small spoons, spinners and plugs had produced only smallish pike and, although the "Jim Vincent" had stirred a couple of better specimens, it was much less productive than the smaller lures.

Harry had also been used to pike fishing in ponds and lakes, usually catching small fish on spoons of various sorts, his biggest being only about 8 pounds although he, too, had lost a monster pike in Carr Mill dam (near St Helens, now filled in), which had taken both the spoon and his end tackle.

We both moved to Dorset and when it came to fishing for pike in rivers, we obviously had to have a rethink. Because of our separate beginnings, and even though we both fish with very similar tackle, we tended to approach our fishing in different ways. Later, we would compare notes, discuss the results, and try to find out why one method was more successful than another.

A rethink on pike

Even a cursory inspection of the angling magazines showed us that most *large* pike were caught by anglers using live or dead fish baits. Was this because of the nature of the baits or was it simply that natural baits were usually larger than artificials? Could it be due to the fact that spinners, spoons and plugs were probably used less often than natural baits? After all, most anglers seem much happier when they are watching a float or bite indicator than using more active methods. There were a number of writers who were enthusiastic lure fishers. Thurlow Craig, in his admirable books *Spinner's Delight* and *Bait Maker's Delight*, described a vast range of lures, some of them obviously practicable and others which had so many joints and hooks that the mere thought of trying to cast them is enough to send a shudder down the spine.

Richard Walker, always a shrewd judge of methods and an advocate of big baits, described in *Still Water Angling* his own failure to catch large pike and his (unusual) lack of success with the species – while at the same time depicting a "wounded rudd" plug and suggesting the possibility of making a replica of a moorhen to attract the big ones.

More recently Barrie Rickards and Ken Whitehead, who are mad keen on spinners, have in their books, like Thurlow Craig before them, gone through long lists of "spinning" lures without solving (at least, to our satisfaction) the problems of *matching* the "natural" for numbers and sizes of pike caught. Perhaps there is no complete answer to the lure *selectivity* puzzle.

To us the obvious approach was to get some reliable information on the behaviour of pike and, in particular, on their eating habits. The pike is a lurking predator; an ambushing, stalking, highly-efficient whiplash of a fish. In some ways, as we have already said, such fish are less easy to catch than freely-swimming hunters. Because of their lurking tactics pike tend to have plenty of time to consider their course of action when they encounter prey. Any spinner, spoon or plug which fails to represent the characteristics of a "food" fish is likely to be rejected out of hand (or should it be out of mouth?).

Food facts

There have been many scientific studies dealing with the food of pike in different waters. It goes without saying that the predators can only feed on fish which are present so, in a northern lough, the only available prey may be countless stunted perch and the young of the pike themselves. In a large Lake District lake enriched by silt, fed by streams draining agricultural land and augmented by sewage effluents, perch may be the *main* food items but roach, charr and trout will supplement the diet. In lowland meres and broads, rudd, tench and bream may become the staple foods, and in rivers the main items will be trout and minnows in the north-west and grayling, dace, roach, chub, barbel, sea trout, salmon, bullheads, gudgeon or minnows elsewhere. The angler must consider matching the shape, form and movement of his lure to the species for which the pike are looking.

The object should be to make sure that the pike recognises the lure as food (it must *look* right), but also to evoke the feeding response by presenting it as a fish isolated from its fellows, showing characteristics of confusion, within easy reach, and slower moving than normal.

It is a well known scientific fact that the largest pike eat the biggest prey. A fish of little more than a yard in length, quite a modest size, could manage a chub of almost half its own length – a fine specimen. Even the largest pike, however, often eat large numbers of prey only two or three inches in length. In waters where minnows are abundant they are usually the most frequent food items of the resident pike of all sizes. This pattern would be more or less typical of pike in a rich lowland river such as the Dorset Stour or in large, hard-water lakes.

So, are the pike selective or are they not? There have been various studies which throw some light on the matter but first, just take an example from a river which we fish for both pike and salmon. Throughout the salmon season every inch of water is combed, almost daily, with a wide range of smallish, artificial lures. Quite often the reward for a hard session of salmon spinning in the frosty conditions of early spring, is a sharp "take" and a brief encounter with two or three pounds of green, glistening, toothy, out of season, disappointment. Most of the pike caught by salmon anglers are small fish in the first two or three years of their lives. Why?

Just to emphasize the point, in the early 1970s we spent a number of years fishing a small river for pike with artificial lures *only*. We used bar-spoons, Tobys and small plugs of various types and the average size of the pike caught was about 3 pounds. Apart from the odd exception (which included a 26-pounder taken on a $2\frac{1}{2}$-inch plastic plug) the biggest specimens landed were only 8–10 pounds in weight and even these were quite rare.

There were probably several reasons for this "lure selectivity". Big pike are numerous in the water fished, because when we switched to the use of live or dead baits, one in four of the pike which we landed was in double figures, with plenty in the upper teens and a sprinkling of twenties. For the moment we will assume that the smaller fish were naive or stupid and the larger ones somehow "educated".

Educated pike

The "catchability" of pike was examined by Dr Beukema, a Dutch scientist, who compared the effect of using spinners with that of small live baits. All the pike caught were immediately returned to the little experimental pond and very few died as a result of being caught. Prior to the experiment the pike used had *never* been angled for, so they were not "educated". Every one of the seventy-nine fish in the pond was tagged so it could be recognised, and the results of the experiment were very revealing.

After about half of the fish had been caught on spinners (Mepps-type bar spoons) they became very difficult to catch by using this method. In contrast, their "catchability" on live baits was not affected by being caught either on spinners or on live fish. Significantly, it proved *extremely* difficult to catch any of the pike *more than once* by spinning, but the fish never seemed to learn about live baits and could be caught again and again.

Despite the fact that pike quickly learn to avoid taking artificials they are (thankfully!) not infallible. In fact, they are suckers compared to some other species of fish. Anyone who looks at the angling magazines will have realised that individual large pike are often caught more than once, particularly by anglers using live or dead fish baits. We have ourselves fished a river in which many of the pike were labelled with numbered jaw tags, and found it possible to catch the same fish over and over again. It can be very impressive to predict to a visiting angler, not only where a fish will take the bait but (as Mike did on one occasion) to say that "it will weigh $17\frac{1}{4}$ pounds"!

Don't bite off more than you can chew!

However, sometimes the catch is not quite what you expect – as Harry found out. It was mid-summer and the River Frome was low and clear. To pass away his lunch hour Harry was hopefully spinning with a small Mepps-Mino on 6-pound nylon with a view to tempting a sea trout, while Mike sat on the bank and criticized his efforts. Suddenly there was a swirl, a flash of metallic green and a tug on the line as a pike of about 2 pounds darted onto the passing lure. Mike watched and chuckled as the little fish kicked and struggled, commenting that "they don't come much smaller than that!" As the words left his lips a fish in the 30-pound class lunged from its resting place in a bed of pond weed and seized the smaller pike square across its great jaws.

Small pike will take big spoons at times

We peered into the depths where we could see the glint of the Mepps blade, still wedged in the scissors of the small fish. As our eyes became accustomed to the shapes we became aware that the head and tail of the "jack" were just showing on either side of its captor's head. Harry quickly flicked off the bale arm of his reel and allowed the line to run freely as the big predator turned away. It moved off a couple of yards and settled down, more or less in its original lair.

Harry opted for a quick strike, fearing that the big fish would nick the fine line with its teeth. He hit the pike as hard as he dared, bending the rod into a deep curve. The massive green shape lifted slowly and moved sedately in the direction of the pull. When it was about five yards from the bank the great jaws yawned wide, releasing their victim. The big pike turned tail and slowly cruised away – the small hook had never even touched its mouth. The problem was, of course, that in the absence of a wire trace Harry had been reluctant to let the monster turn its prey and although, in this case, the attraction was natural rather than artificial, this problem lies at the heart of all freshwater spinning where pike are present. (I *do* wish that Harry would sometimes follow my advice, so generously offered.)

The large size of a pike's mouth, and the uncompromising nature of its attack, makes it liable to engulf any small lure. Once inside that roomy interior it becomes only a matter of time until the line contacts the fish's personal set of needle-like nylon cutters. Here lies the only real difference between spinning for pike and for other freshwater species. If you are to avoid frequent lure losses it will be necessary to

1 link the lure to the main line with a few inches of wire, or
2 use a lure big enough to stand a fair chance of separating the line from the pike's teeth.

No experienced pike spinner is likely to be unaware of the danger of "bite-offs". A couple of examples will serve to illustrate the point. While Mike was fishing for salmon with a small Canadian Wiggler (a metal "flatfish" lure) in the clear waters of the Dorset Frome a pike, well into double figures, shot out from the bank beneath his feet. The lure disappeared into its mouth and without the slightest snatch, tug or pluck, it left him with the 12-pound B.S. nylon fluttering from the rod top.

On a second occasion Mike was fishing with a large "Jim Vincent" spoon tied direct to 18-pound B.S. A tiny jack pike of about a pound attacked the lure, missed it completely and sheared through the line just above the lure, which sank to the river bed in six feet of water. When the spoon was subsequently retrieved (after much prodding about with the rod top) the knot was intact and the line was cut, as though by scissors. When fishing unknown water, even if the presence of pike is in doubt, it is advisable to use a wire trace. (If only Mike would *listen* to me this would never have happened!)

Pike, American style

Further information is available from the North Americans, who have several species of pike in their waters. The two of most interest are the northern pike (our own *Esox lucius*), and the larger and even more desirable muskellunge (*Esox masquinongy*). Two scientists, Weittman and Anderson, stocked eight small ponds with these fish to see whether one species was easier to catch than the other. Two ponds had only pike, two had only muskies, two had tiger muskies (a cross between the two species) and in the last two ponds were a mixture of all three.

In fifty-eight hours of spinning with Mepps spinners, spread equally between ponds, fifty-nine fish were caught. Two-thirds of those caught were pike and the rest were about equal numbers of musky and tiger musky.

Of the twenty (northern) pike in the ponds every one was caught at least once and one was caught seven times! The scientists said that the pike were about *four times* easier to catch on Mepps than muskies and three times easier than tigers. Fish were handled many times but very few died due to hooking. Three deeply-hooked fish recovered and survived.

The pike has millions of years of natural selection behind its ability to distinguish the edible from the inedible. Each year's crop of young and inexperienced pike contains a share of the slow, the short-sighted, the unlucky and the downright gormless. These unfortunates fall prey, at first to fierce predatory insects, then to larger fish, birds and ultimately to pike anglers. Once these simpletons have been weeded out or "educated" to the dangers which lie in depending only on simple flash or vibration to signal *food*, they become much more difficult to tempt. Anything about a lure which does not look fully acceptable as a food object may cause it to be inspected and then rejected. Spinning for pike, depending upon the circumstances and whether the pike are "educated" or not, can be very rewarding or very discouraging. All we can say is, give it a try and find out how easy it is to catch the pike in your area.

Mike with a 30 pound pike taken on a large (Jim Vincent) spoon. Note the February flood conditions.

CHAPTER EIGHT

SEA FISH

The fussy pollack

Spinning for sea fish is a neglected angling science but, for any species which takes moving prey or feeds in the company of others of its kind, a lure of the right size, shape, colour and action can produce hectic sport. So, once again, what is the right lure? It changes not only from pollack to cod or from bass to mackerel but also with the time of year, with the age and size of the fish and with the fishing conditions. (If fishing were easy, and success assured, few of us would remain hooked on angling!)

A detailed example of such a change in diet with the *age* of the fish has been described by Drs Potts and Wooton of the Marine Biological Association at Plymouth. This information deals only with pollack and we will use it to show how the best time, place and method for catching a species alters completely as the fish increase in size. A similar sequence of changes also applies to most other predatory sea fish.

Baby pollack, when they first appear inshore, usually in very shallow water or in estuaries, feed mainly on tiny crustaceans which they pick from seaweeds or catch in open water. When the fish reach about 6 inches long (just the size when they can become a nuisance to anglers after bigger game, and when they can first be caught on a tiny, jigged lure or fly) they switch from crustacea to feeding on two-spot gobies. The gobies are, at most, $2\frac{1}{2}$ inches in length and unlike others of their kind they swim near the surface of the sea around beds of wrack, kelp or eel grass. Often the little gobies shoal-up tightly over small clearings in the weedbeds and to catch them the pollack have to change their hunting tactics

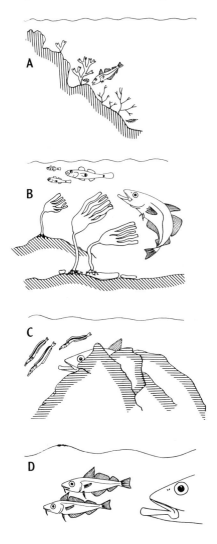

Figure 7
Changes in feeding behaviour of pollack with age. **A** Young fish feed on small crustaceans. **B** Fish take two-spot gobies from kelp beds. **C** Pollack ambush sand eels from cover. **D** Large fish hunt actively for poor cod and greater sand eels.

to a pursuit method. This is very successful because the pollack are much faster and more powerful swimmers than the gobies.

Soon the young pollack, which are growing quickly, need a more plentiful supply of food and to obtain it they switch their diet again, this time to baby lesser-sand-eels which, in the hours of daylight, swim and feed in huge numbers over inshore sandy bottoms. Unfortunately for the young pollack the sand eels are much faster and more alert than the two-spot gobies and the pursuit tactic no longer works. The pollack are not slow to learn and they resort to stalking the sand eels from the cover of rocky outcrops. Any patch of rock, located on a sandy sea bed, however small, will form a territory for pollack, and such cover is so desirable that the fish will actually defend their territory from other pollack which might compete with them for food.

In the course of the summer the young pollack grow until they are a foot or more in length; quite big enough to provide interesting sport on light tackle. (Ask Jim Churchouse and the youngsters of Weymouth Angling Club – they are experts!) By now the tiny sand eels are no longer adequate food so the solitary, stalking tactic is changed and the fish gather into feeding schools, swimming in mid-water. These hunting shoals chase after various species of mid-water forage fish, particularly the large greater-sand-eels. The pollack are much more versatile now and will raid the inshore reefs for small "rock-fish"; pouting, poor-cod and other prey species are all taken with characteristic lunging ferocity.

It is at this stage that the larger specimens move out into deeper water to shoal over rocky pinnacles and wrecks. In the autumn and early winter, when rough seas pound the coast, these lunkers will sometimes visit inshore grounds and, from our local beaches such as Chesil and Durdle Door, most years see the capture of a few fish well into double figures at this time. In late winter the big fish gather on offshore marks to spawn, often in company with large coalfish, and it is then that the Redgill, Eddystone or live sand-eel on a flowing trace, is likely to produce that "fish of a life-time" for those with the enthusiasm, cash and stomach to go afloat.

Pollack time

By examining the gut contents of captured pollack (or for that matter, of any other fish) it is possible to get some idea of *when* the fish are most likely to feed. Fresh, new, prey appear in pollack guts most often in the early morning round about first light. Later in the day the stomachs mostly contain well-digested prey. The fish will also feed actively at dusk, which is the time when we have often caught large numbers by spinning with "rubber" eels, long slim spoons, pirks, plugs or flies.

In relation to shore fishing for pollack, Mike well remembers his first experiences of catching these fish on lures. He was on a late summer holiday in the Isle of Man and his favourite fishing spot was the rugged, volcanic peninsula of Langness point in the south-east of the island. Wrasse and pollack were abundant in the deep, weedy gulleys and, with his pal Bob Sprawling, Mike would spend the entire day float fishing or paternostering for these fish with rag, lug or crab baits.

On the morning of the day in question, the wind had shifted overnight and when they reached their favoured gulley a gale of rough, cold air from the south-west was buffeting the rods as they tackled up. Six hours and a couple of small wrasse later they had almost given up hope of any reasonable catch. Cold and miserable, they decided to opt for shelter in the last hour of daylight. Picking up the gear they crossed the short sea turf to the east side of the peninsula. As they scrambled down to the water level the protection of the high rocky walls began to have its effect and the calm surface of the water within the deep gulley was a complete contrast to their previous pitch. Ten yards out the flat surface was suddenly broken as, with a plop, a 10-inch pollack flung itself into the air. Instantly their attitude changed and they dug about in the tackle bag for something to attract the fish. Thinking that the pollack which had shown itself was likely to be typical of others present, they tied small Toby spoons to their 10-pound lines.

Even in those days (the 1950s) the standard spinning rods were Mark IV carp rods, home-made from split cane, cut and glued in the workshop (kitchen). Built for coping with

20-pound plus carp, the rods were very powerful weapons and Bob and Mike were confident of dealing with pollack of any size in the twenty feet of water. On the first cast they realised that their confidence was misplaced. Bob's Toby was grabbed almost as it hit the water and the fish "sounded" for the bottom. A string of expletives greeted the dive as his rod crashed round into its fighting curve and the clutch screamed and released line.

The steady pressure began to tell and shortly a $3\frac{1}{2}$-pound, olive-gold, wet-look pollack was flapping at the surface. As it was unhooked and returned, Mike struck into his own crash-diver and time and again their rods plunged towards the

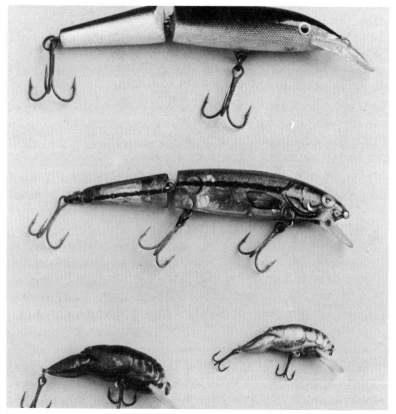

Some buoyant plugs which are extremely effective for sea fish. The two upper lures are excellent for catching bass and pollack in shallow, snaggy conditions. The lower "Crayfish" plugs are particularly good for wrasse in deeper water.

water as fish after fish, ranging from a pound to over 6 pounds, mistook the little flickering spoons for small fry.

In fact, despite the powerful tackle, they lost several large fish which made unstoppable dives for the refuge of the kelp stems. This habit of the pollack, of making a smart vertical dive is, of course, well known to wreck anglers. Even large pollack can be landed from quite shallow water when wrack, rather than kelp, is the main form of weed.

The possibility of big pollack from shallow water was again brought home to Mike on Langness point, when he encountered one of the local lighthouse keepers carrying a stout bamboo pole (like a carpenter stiffener), terminating in a length of fixed line, down to a shallow rocky cleft. He struck up a conversation and they walked together down to the sea. The heavy nylon tied to the end of the pole was armed with a hefty weight and three good-sized, white-feathered lures.

The lighthouseman proceeded to work the lures, sink and draw, in the three or four feet of water covering a meadow of serrated wrack on the sea bed. The tide was flooding quickly into the cleft and, as Mike watched, a bronze torpedo flashed from the wrack thicket and impaled itself on one of the feathered hooks. In short order a double-figure pollack was heaved onto the rocks and despatched. Two other fish, only a little smaller than the first, followed quickly and it was clear from the angler's manner and his comments that he had done it all before. Mike never managed to catch a pollack of over 10 pounds from the shallows, despite the lighthouse keeper's tuition, but on a number of occasions the sport with fish of 5-pounds plus was spectacular. Before the accidental meeting he had never dreamed of catching such large fish from water scarcely deep enough to cover their backs. Many times since he has realised what he had been missing.

Coalfish, the pollack of the north

Pollack of various sizes provide sport for experienced anglers and practice for the less experienced around the south and west coasts of Britain but, in the north and east, coalfish play the same part. Young coalfish (up to three years of age) will, like the pollack, take feathers and spinning lures. Mike recalls feathering from the stone pier at Craster, Northumberland, and catching one "podley" (coalfish) after another. The biggest were 3–4 pounds in weight, but most of them were younger fish of about $1\frac{1}{2}$ pounds.

A small pirk or a willow-leaf spoon is also very effective for coalies. Coalfish are generally regarded as second-class fish in the north-east, with cod and codling being the prime choice. In years past, both spinning and fly fishing for coalfish were quite popular and off the rugged scars at Filey Brigg surface-feeding coalfish were often caught by these methods in August and September every year.

Coalfish are generally very obliging. Even younger specimens eat lots of fish and will readily take lures. We have caught literally thousands of second- and third-year specimens from the quays and rock edges of Northumberland and Berwickshire. In suitably calm, warm evening conditions it may be possible to take a "fish a cast" on light spinning tackle. Larger coalfish are often caught on trolled lures intended for mackerel. Mike recalls vividly that, when he was a youngster, he went fishing with John Harper, a friend of his parents, out of Castletown, Isle of Man. The basic idea was to troll a conventional "spinner" for mackerel on the way out to the cod banks and then to jig with a "murderer" for cod over the banks themselves. Both of these tactics produced large pollack and coalfish.

One of Mike's strongest memories is of the excitement in the boat when the heavy, hemp mackerel line in his hand yanked tight and a strenuous tug-of-war resulted in the gaffing of a 12-pound coalfish which, at the time, was the biggest fish he had caught. It took a mackerel spinner garnished with a silver sweet-wrapper, which started him on a fashion which took years to break. Modern sand-eel imitations, spoons and plugs are even more effective attractors of large coalfish and pollack and the use of Redgill or Eddystone-style eels on flying collar rigs over wrecks and reefs at spawning time is now a well known tactic.

We have lift-off!

Both species tend to strike at lures from below and, in doing so, may literally rocket from the water as they overshoot the bait. We have both seen such behaviour and there are many examples of this sort of action in the angling literature. Holcombe, in 1921, wrote – "a number of big pollack suddenly made their appearance in the wake of the boat, tumbling over and over one another for all the world like a school of porpoises and one fish (of some 9lb or 10lb) was actually gaffed into the boat close to the rudder."

Another classic example was described to us in 1984 in a letter from Mike Browning of Milford Haven, Wales. Mike spends a lot of time trolling with Redgill lures for bass but he is keen to try other lures which might improve results. He writes as follows and we give the full account to show the possibilities of lure fishing:

I fished all day with a large sinking Rapala (mackerel type). Not a fish looked at it. At the end of the day – dusk falling – I decided to head for home. I opened up the engine and, in a filthy temper, reeled in the plug as fast as possible. As it came to the surface I saw a large mouth behind it which enveloped the lure within a foot of the surface. The fish (a porbeagle I think) then turned, causing a torrent of water to pour over me! I returned to the harbour wet and very thoughtful, and poorer by the £5 cost of the Rapala.

On the second occasion we were trolling with Redgills and plugs, but the "driver" placed his rod down so that he could concentrate on steering in a dangerous area. His lure, a large Rapala, was bobbing about in the wake of the boat about one yard back from the propeller. Three of us in the stern saw a large pollack appear from the depths and try to seize the lure – it missed but the force of its pursuit carried it several feet above the surface. It was at least ten pounds.

Presumably the fish are attracted to the bubbles and cavitation effects in the wake of boats. The many silvery reflections may well resemble shoals of small bait fish, suggesting that a hose played onto the water surface in late evening might drive pollack and coalfish into a feeding frenzy.

The cod, a sociable feeder

Cod are themselves almost as predatory as their sleeker cousins already mentioned and they often swim in schools. In the case of small fish this is a method of predator defence but the bigger fish will gather together for feeding. These feeding groups are believed to be rather loose and widely scattered with the fish barely in sight of one another. When one fish finds food, its behaviour, twisting, turning and flashing, will attract its neighbours to the area. Schools of cod, and other fish, are mainly kept together by sight and this is where the lure fisherman can score.

As we have said, cod are attracted by the flash and movement of other feeding fish. The signal sent out by a large swinging spoon or side-slipping pirk serves a double purpose. First, it will attract any cod within viewing range and second, it will look like food as the fish close in.

Cod have large and well developed eyes which they use to good advantage. At one time scientists believed that these fish were so dependent on vision that they were unable to feed in the dark. However, they have since been shown to catch living food even in the total gloom of a photographic darkroom. Fish "tagged" with tiny ultrasonic transmitters in their stomachs remained almost stationary in the hours of daylight even in the dim light of 50-foot depth.

Pirking progress

In the early 1950s many fishermen used to fish for cod with "murderers", the forerunners of modern pirks. The murderers were heavy pieces of lead-filled metal pipe or lead bars fitted with big single hooks. The surfaces of the lures were polished or scraped with a knife until they shone and the heavyweight attractors were jigged up and down on hefty hand lines. The cod were hooked either in the mouth or, quite often, in the outside of the jaws or head. Some very big cod were caught by this method and no doubt it would still be effective, but for angling (and commercial fishing) purposes they have now been succeeded by the jigs and pirks introduced from North America and Scandinavia.

The principle of jigging is best applied in situations where the angler can fish, more or less, straight up and down into relatively deep water. The obvious places from which to use jigs and pirks are boats, either drifting or at anchor, from steep rock marks or from piers and jetties. We have tried them from all these places with success. Any sort of predatory fish may be caught by jigging – the method was not designed for cod alone.

Off the Pacific coast of Canada and the USA salmon are the main quarry of anglers jigging from steep rocky shores. They use a wide variety of pirks (they call them "diamond jigs"), many of them resembling the familiar Prisma. Some are drilled and slide freely on the line above the hook. There is probably not much to choose between the various types. The standard tactics involve a spinning rod (about 2-pound test curve), 12–15-pound line and a fixed spool reel with a large capacity: a 40-pound king (chinook) salmon with the entire Pacific Ocean in front of it can take a bit of stopping! When Mike tried the methods out during a brief business visit to British Columbia he was entertained by two huge sea-lions which were clearly after the same prey. He caught only a single 7-pound coho, or blackmouth salmon, using a white $1\frac{1}{2}$ ounce pirk called a "Polar Bear". The rocks from which he

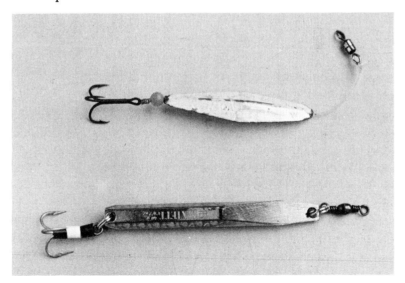

Two of the many types of pirk used for jigging or long casting in the sea. The upper lure is a Canadian "Polar Bear" and the lower lure is the ABU Sextett.

fished fell away into such a depth of water that he *never* managed to "find bottom" despite allowing the lure to sink with almost all of his 200 yards of line.

In Britain we have used pirks from piers and dinghies to catch cod, mackerel, pollack, coalfish, pouting, garfish and bass. It is often productive and convenient to fish a small silver pirk while waiting for a "run" on conventional bottom tackle. The idea is to "find" the sea bed by lowering the pirk and then to work it steadily back towards the water surface, sink and draw, until the fish are located. Remember that the fish will generally be nearer the surface at dawn and dusk, particularly in settled, warm, calm weather.

The Danes and Norwegians often fish almost exclusively with pirks. Like the Canadian salmon anglers, they jig from steep rocks into deep water for cod, coalfish and torsk. The technique involves a terminal jigging lure and a couple of droppers with plastic shrimps or squids – a good method to use when exploring new territory. The main lure can act either as a flasher to attract and stimulate predators to take small accessory lures, or as a fish catcher in its own right.

Bass – shallow water specialists

Around the south and west coasts of the British Isles the main summer species is the bass. Unlike the fish mentioned previously bass are *really* at home in shallow water and often need a different approach. At the opposite extreme to the heavy, vertical-fishing, deep-water lures discussed so far, are the ultra-light surface plug baits. Buoyant plugs can be designed to fish at almost any depth, but among the most useful are those which dive only a few inches or, at most, a foot or two beneath the surface. Fast tides, shallow water and snaggy seabeds are the conditions under which these most fish-like objects come into their own. Bass, wrasse, pollack and mackerel are all susceptible to these versatile lures.

Buoyant plugs are almost all armed with two or three treble hooks which makes them liable to rake up every fragment of weed or rubbish from the water, but there is one massive advantage of this arrangement. The middle hooks are ideally placed to take side-smashing predators such as bass or pollack, while the tail treble will often nick into the rubbery lips of a wrasse or even a mullet which is trying to nip its tail.

Perhaps the best way to impress the advantages of using floating plugs is to describe a typical trip to our own stretch of the Dorset coast. It was mid-summer and, with our pals Terry Gledhill and Martin Williams, we had decided to make the pilgrimage to St Aldhelm's Head. It was a fine, bright, sunny day as we scrambled down the shaley slope to the sea. This was followed by twenty minutes exhausting progress over large rugged boulders. As we reached the Head, the tide was flooding and the fierce race was churning up white tops two hundred yards offshore.

We selected our personal boulders and each began to cast the lure of his choice. Mike and Martin clipped on heavy spoons and tried to belt them out to the edge of the race where the occasional mackerel could be seen leaping into the air. The other two tried plug fishing closer inshore, Terry with a big greenish Rebel and Harry with a Rapala J11. The early action was limited to a couple of mackerel hooked, and just as quickly lost, at maximum range.

After about an hour Martin switched to a Rapala and was quickly into a wrasse of reasonable size. As he hooked the fish he gave a shout and Mike laid down his rod and clambered across to help land it (the boulders being rugged and awkward). As they jointly pinned down, unhooked and returned the 3-pound copper and yellow prize, Terry, perched on the biggest boulder in sight, shouted "Fish!" They looked up to see his Milbro-Ghillie salmon spinning rod well bent towards the sea.

Mike, already rodless, picked up the communal landing-net and, again scrambling from rock to rock, went to Terry's assistance. He scaled the big boulder just as the grey and silver shape of a decent bass tore off on another run. The water boiled as the fish's tail swept from side to side and pushed it towards a gap in the kelp. Terry swung the rod over to the side and steered his bass away from trouble. The fish plunged and thrashed but now there was no escape from the nylon filament. It was drawn towards the rocks and into the folds of the waiting net. That fine bass weighed $6\frac{1}{2}$lb.

In fishing for bass, particularly from steep rocks into deeper water, mackerel, garfish and scad are all potential catches on lures. Our experience suggests that, despite their reputations as easy catches, all three can be distinctly fussy about what they eat.

An 11 pound 4 ounce bass in fine condition. The fish was caught on a buoyant Rapala plug.

The fastidious mackerel

Mackerel will, without doubt, take almost anything that moves *when they are in a feeding frenzy*. Because of this and because of their desirability as bait the methods developed for their capture are decidedly crude. Feathers tied on hooks stout enough for skate or conger are jigged or trailed on strings of nylon-monofilament thick enough to cope with "Jaws". Why is it that a species of fish the size of dace or roach is so suicidal? Even using a string of feathers, it is often obvious that one lure is favoured by the fish. This is particularly clear if a small spoon or mackerel spinner is tied to the end of the string and if the mackerel are few and far between. The metal lure will frequently outfish the feathers ten to one. A small strip of mackerel skin will also enhance the attraction of a lure, so even in the turmoil of thrashing fish and whisking hooks the mackerel are able to pick and choose.

Three further lessons may be learned from the mackerel enthusiasts.

1 Multi-lured tackles will attract fish to the area.
2 A hooked fish will attract others to neighbouring lures, and
3 a thick line and traces do not always deter fish from biting.

The selective ability of mackerel soon becomes apparent when float-fished baits are used to catch them. Many years ago, when Mike fished for mackerel at Plymouth under the tuition of local experts, he was shown how even a carefully trimmed strip of mackerel skin was inferior to freshly caught 'brit' when it came to producing bites.

In terms of spinning we have landed mackerel on most types of lure. Flies, plugs, bar-spoons, spoons, spinners, pirks and even hookless lead weights on a couple of occasions, have all tempted fish. Nevertheless, the basic principles of spinning with artificials should be followed. The movement, size, shape, colour and swimming depth of the natural food (usually small, silvery fish) should be copied as closely as possible.

A mackerel caught on a "Polar Bear" pirk. The lure slides freely on the line like a devon minnow.

At dusk the fish and their prey tend to gather near the sea surface, particularly in periods of warm, calm weather, and this is where to seek them. Often the spots where they congregate are quite local and can only be learned by experience. Deep-water races are pretty reliable but even quite shallow, sheltered bays will sometimes prove productive, a good example being the shingly, cliff-bound cove of Chapman's Pool in Dorset where we have often caught these fish.

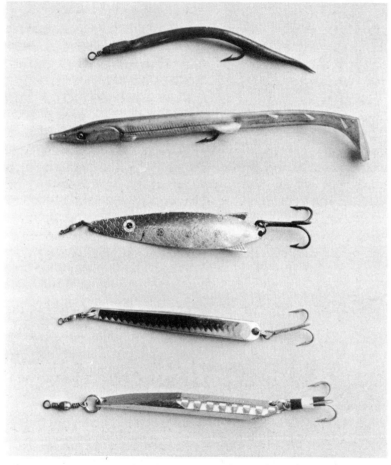

Rubber eels and spoons widely used for sea fishing. The rubber eel (top) has largely been superseded by the "Red Gill" type eel below it. The metal lures provide weight for casting, but because of their design and weight the bottom two lures must be retrieved much more quickly than the "Toby" spoon.

Again in our area, the famous Chesil Beach is noted as a source of mackerel in abundance. Most are caught by long casters using heavy leads and feathers, but spinning gear and a single lure will also give sport – if you can find enough elbow room to use them without being anti-social to the "serious" fishermen!

This brings us to the question of catching mackerel on single lures. The two main characteristics of the species to be considered are its vitality and its brittle mouth. Many angling writers have commented on the fighting qualities of these little fish, but relatively few anglers take advantage of this "sport potential" in choosing their tackle. Trolling under power makes it practically impossible to fish with sensible gear. The drag on spinning tackle at a trolling speed of only $1\frac{1}{2}$ knots is ridiculous and, when a fish is hooked, most of the fight is hauled out of it before the "way" has been taken off the boat. The only way to appreciate the power of these mini-tuna is to fish from the shore or from a stationary or drifting boat. A lure appropriate to the conditions and swimming depth of the fish, cast or jigged on 7- or 8-pound line, will provide fantastic sport. Why such heavy line? The brittle mouth of the fish gives no sound hold for tiny hooks and a sensible compromise is a fair-sized (2, 4 or 6) treble or single and a rod and line suitable to hook the fish firmly.

Garfish and scad

Both garfish and scad are, at times, caught by anglers fishing for mackerel and indeed the three species have much in common, though neither is quite such a sucker for artificial lures as the mackerel itself. The mere shape of the gar's mouth is enough to suggest that it might be difficult to hook – and indeed it is; often breaking free after a few lightning rushes or a skittering leap. The scad is less of a fish-eater than either of the others and is much more likely to fall to float-fished worm baits. Even scad, however, can be caught in very large numbers by spinning methods. On one occasion Harry landed one scad after another on a small bar-spoon. He was fishing from the shingle beach of Chapman's Pool in the late evening in September; all were returned alive to the water.

Save our sea fish

These are the main species of predatory sea fish taken on lures around our coasts. The tackle and tactics used are not very different from those which catch game and coarse fish in rivers and lakes. The basic idea is to fish with rod, reel and line appropriate to the conditions being fished, using lures designed to attract the species which is sought. Sea fish are no easier and no more difficult to catch than any others and, to succeed, everything needs to be correct. When success comes, because many species form large schools, it may be very, very satisfying.

Spinning for sea fish is *exactly* the same as spinning for coarse or game fish. If there are no fish you will not catch any! If the conditions are wrong you will not catch any! If you are using a lure which is unsuitable you will have very few bites! However, before we end this chapter, we feel obliged to make a serious plea to all anglers. If you are fortunate enough to find the correct combination of fish, conditions, lures, tackle and tactics you may be able to catch very large numbers of fish. If you need them to eat, to feed your family or to fill your freezer with food or bait, fair enough – but please return unwanted fish to the sea. If you dump them on the beach, bury them in the garden or even sell them for profit, then you are endangering the future of angling as a sport. Quite apart from the possible depletion of stocks by your efforts, there are those who (wrongly, in our view) see angling as a cruel and greedy sport. We should do nothing to encourage this impression.

CHAPTER NINE

SALMON FACTS AND FIGURES

A spring salmon

It was a pleasant, mild, sunny April day of the kind peculiar to south Dorset. Mike had been hoeing and weeding between the rows of peas on his small allotment and as he walked up the short road to his parked car he felt well satisfied with his efforts. Parked beside his car he found the familiar shape of the Vauxhall Chevette belonging to Jon Bass. Mike recalled that it was Jon's salmon fishing day and, before driving home, he decided to walk across the field to a spot from which he had a good view of the river. The chances of seeing any action as a result of this impulse were very small but, as luck would have it, he could just see a figure on the bank about a quarter of a mile upstream.

Being rather short-sighted Mike could not make out what was going on; however, there was something not quite right. Why was he (assuming that the figure *was* Jon) standing on the concreted area just upstream of the big gauging weir? Even if he was fishing in that unlikely spot, why did he not move on? With an angler's instinct Mike decided to walk up and see what was happening.

As he approached the weir it became apparent that Jon was not in fact casting and retrieving but standing quite still, rod held aloft, and bent towards some object in the river. Mike broke into a trot and, as he crossed the bridge over the weir, he shouted "What is it?" above the noise of the rushing water. At that moment Jon was too occupied to reply, but when he reached his side the picture became clear.

The fish had been hooked one hour earlier and about thirty yards further upstream. It had been immediately obvious that this was a very large salmon and, apart from one possible gaffing opportunity in the first couple of minutes, it had remained deep, swimming slowly upstream and then back down again until now it rested under the far bank, a yard or two above the weir.

Mike lay down on the bridge and peered into the depths. The 3-inch wooden yellow-belly was clearly visible as it turned slowly on the trace two feet beneath the surface. Three feet deeper, just above the gravel bed, he could see the faint grey shape of a big spring fish, its great fan of a tail waving gently as it effortlessly held station against the strong flow. After a brief consultation it was decided that Mike should try to persuade the fish to go upstream, away from the hazard of the concrete weir-supports, but he was unable to reach far enough down with the gaff to disturb it.

Eventually the fish itself decided to go for another leisurely swim upstream. Hugging the river bed it covered about fifty or sixty yards, during which they had only an occasional, tantalising glimpse of a broad back. Jon tried to apply a little more pressure; the salmon, clearly irritated by this tension, once again turned downstream. This time there was a purposeful air about its movements and, despite Jon's efforts to apply sidestrain, it headed straight for the central arch of the bridge over the weir. All attempts to retard its progress were in vain and, as it became obvious that the salmon was about to descend into the weir pool (at its second attempt), Jon opened the bale arm of his reel. Taking the gaff, Mike ran to the centre of the bridge and hooked up the nylon line. Once the line was firmly in his grasp Jon re-engaged the bale arm and consigned his well worn rod and reel to the river. Hand over hand Mike hauled the rod and reel through the arch, carefully hoisted it onto the bridge and handed it back into Jon's eager grasp. He reeled up the slack line; the fish was still attached, and after a few words with Mike he decided to go down the north bank, thus avoiding a large hawthorn bush on the south bank of the pool.

The fish circled slowly, deep in the race, and they were

both confident it would be played out and landed in this arena.

In the following half-hour it threatened once to ascend the weir but was dissuaded by heavy sidestrain. Twice it rushed to the far side of the race, a distance of about thirty yards, and hurled itself clear of the water – a stupendous sight which brought gasps from them both.

Clearly the salmon was now tiring and, as is often the case with a weakened fish, it began to move downstream, using its massive flank to broadside the current. Jon had little control in the strong flow but he was still confident that he would be able to coax it within reach of the gaff before long. It surged downstream under the far bank with the two of them walking abreast of it. The first doubts began to creep into their minds as they approached an impassable ditch on their bank some 400 yards downstream of the weir pool. It was now or never! Jon tried to bully the fish across to the slack water at the end of the ditch but it gained a new lease of life and started into a powerful downstream run. Jon's face lengthened and grew pale as sixty yards of line were dragged off under maximum pressure. They were stranded at the end of the ditch and, unless the fish stopped, all was lost.

As though in answer to a prayer, far downstream the salmon made its third leap and thankfully the run stopped. Jon was left with the problem of what to do. Any attempt to drag the fish back upstream could trigger off another potentially disastrous run. It was obvious that they had to cross to the other bank of the river but the only crossing point was the bridge, a quarter-of-a-mile upstream. Mike began to run up the bank, pounded over the bridge, and raced down the south side of the river.

When he arrived opposite the ditch, gasping for breath, he was relieved to hear that the fish had not moved. Javelin style, Jon risked all and threw the rod, butt first, across the river. Mike picked it up, still in one piece, closed the bale arm and began to wind up the slack line while Jon threw the gaff after the rod and set off on the long run.

Waders and waterproofs are not the ideal kit for a sharp sprint and, with Jon still far upstream, Mike had recovered all the slack. He held his breath and peeked over the edge of the bank where the line disappeared. There it was! A huge submarine of a fish resting just beneath the surface, close under the bank, in a small reed-fringed inlet well within reach of the 4-foot gaff. He glanced upstream again. Jon was still minutes away. What if the fish set off downstream again? There was an impassable road bridge a little further down. He made his decision, took the rubber off the point of the gaff and crept back to the bank.

It was all over in a couple of seconds; the gaff went home by the dorsal fin and he dragged the fish onto the bank and well away from the water's edge. He looked up apprehensively, wondering how his pal, still some distance away, would react to his actions. Jon slowed down to a walk and his sigh of relief was distinctly audible, even at that distance.

A couple of minutes later, when they had both recovered their breath, they stood drooling over the mighty fish and speculating on its weight. A check on Jon's watch showed that the entire struggle had lasted three-and-a-quarter hours. The sun was going down as they took it in turns to carry the fish back to the car. The spring balance registered exactly $34\frac{1}{2}$ pounds; the biggest from the beat for many years and a fantastic experience for them both.

Even taking into account its size this fish took an exceptionally long time to land – chiefly because of the circumstances

Ian Farr (6′ 4½″ tall) with a fresh-run spring salmon, from the river Frome, weighing 24 pounds. The fish took a wooden devon minnow (blue/silver).

under which it was caught. We have known other salmon, not much smaller, to virtually give themselves up within minutes. In fact, experience suggests that the best and most exciting battles were usually with small- to medium-sized salmon caught when the river was heavily weeded.

Unfortunately, there is not much information available on the time taken to play and land individual fish so, since it is always of interest to compare angling results with those of other fishermen, we have tried a different approach. The catches of nine anglers (we are amongst them) are compared over a period of nine consecutive years. All fished on the same beat and, in any year, each was permitted (but did not always take advantage of) an equal share of fishing time. First, we considered the number of salmon which they caught. As you might expect, there were good years and bad years for everyone. In some cases, indicated in the Table by a dash, the person did not fish in that year. In 1976, a severe drought year, only eleven salmon were caught by the seven anglers, whereas in 1981 forty-three fish were landed by nine. Only three anglers (1, 3 and 8) ever managed a double figure season's catch. A second table shows the fishing effort, in rod hours, required for an angler to catch a salmon on this beat. Also shown are the total number of fish caught by each and the rod hours per fish in his worst years.

It is striking that the number of rod hours fished over the nine years ranged from 203 (angler 9) to 579 (angler 8) (roughly a three-fold difference); the number of fish caught varied from 7 (angler 7) to 43 (angler 8) (about six-fold). Generally, the anglers spending least time on the river caught the least fish. Perhaps the most surprising fact is that the effort needed to catch a fish (by a given angler) was very consistent. For example, anglers 4 and 6 appeared to be the most efficient and, year in year out, averaged only 9.7 to 11.6 hours per fish; while angler 7, despite putting in roughly the same amount of total time, needed four or five times as long to catch a fish. The other anglers fell somewhere between these extremes. The reasons for such big differences are by no means clear. Obviously luck plays a very small part, otherwise the results for a given angler would vary a lot more.

The best lies are "common knowledge" so simply knowing which bits of river are productive is of little value. This leaves two features of obvious importance. First, the more efficient anglers probably concentrated their efforts in periods when fish were relatively thick on the ground. Second, to average one fish per ten-to-twelve hours it must have been necessary to make the most of every chance; few fish would have been lost and a minimum number of takes missed.

To anglers who have fished for salmon on a top Scottish or Irish river, ten-hours-per-fish must seem pretty grim. However, the river in question is a chalk stream with an annual run of about 2000 salmon and a rod catch of about 200. The beat fished is roughly a mile-and-a-half long and is only one

Table 1. Number of salmon caught per year

Year	1973	74	75	76	77	78	79	80	81
1	10	0	2	2	5	2	–	2	9
2	2	4	2	1	3	6	2	5	4
3	5	1	3	2	5	2	1	1	11
4	7	4	4	2	1	1	6	6	4
5	2	2	2	–	2	–	1	5	1
6	8	8	4	1	5	0	–	–	2
7	–	1	1	0	0	1	1	2	1
8	–	4	16	3	1	3	5	3	8
9	–	0	1	–	0	0	3	3	3
Total	34	24	35	11	22	15	19	27	43

Table 2. Fishing effort in rod hours

Angler	Total fish (9 years)	Total hours fished	(Rod hours/fish) Average year	Best year	Worst year
1	32	381	11.9	10.4	14.0
2	29	561	19.3	17.2	21.8
3	31	420	13.5	13.1	17.9
4	35	374	10.7	9.7	11.1
5	15	240	16.0	14.9	19.9
6	28	308	11.0	10.6	11.6
7	7	305	43.6	41.1	54.4
8	43	579	13.5	12.0	16.0
9	10	203	20.3	17.8	26.0

of many similar stretches, but it produces twelve to thirteen per cent of the catch for the whole river.

With regard to fishing at the "best" time of the year; this can be very variable. Generally, May, June and July are the most productive months while March and April produce fewer fish. However, the "spring" fish caught in the latter months are usually large salmon of 15–25 pounds. Some anglers are prepared to put in many cold and fruitless hours in the hope of catching a spring monster. (One local angler of our acquaintance had the fantastic experience of landing, in the space of a few weeks in early spring, three salmon, each weighing over 30 pounds.)

Finally, we examined the catch figures to see which methods had been used most successfully.

Table 3. Salmon caught on different baits over 7 years

Year	1973	1974	1975	1976	1977	1978	1979
Devon	9	2	5	1	7	4	2
Mepps	–	1	–	3	1	–	–
Plug	–	2	–	–	2	5	9
Other (fly, prawn, worm etc.)	25	19	30	7	12	6	8

It would appear that the light-weight devons were the most effective "spinning" lures on this river. However, this is not really a fair comparison because Water Authority bye-laws ban the use of plugs, prawns and worms for the first two-and-a-half months of the season. Against this, devons are being used early in the year when less fish are present in the river. On the whole the table probably gives a reasonable picture. Devons are undoubtedly the *easiest* lures to use effectively of those which *are* permitted at that time of year. If plugs were permitted they would certainly catch their fair share of large spring fish.

In conclusion, although a certain amount of knowledge of the nature of a good salmon "lie" can be an advantage, anyone with experience of spinning for other species of fish can be confident of catching a salmon on spinning gear, providing they have (a) the time to spare and (b) access to a salmon river where spinning is allowed.

CHAPTER TEN

SPINNING FOR SALMON

A spring salmon angler

It was the first day of March and rain was driving horizontally into Harry's face as he trudged along the river bank through brown, muddy pools deeply churned by the hooves of drinking cattle. A stronger gust of wind briefly halted his progress and sent a flurry of icy water from the cuff of his waterproof jacket into the open end of the sleeve, where it trickled from his rod-hand, down his forearm and onto his flexed elbow.

By the NO FISHING sign which marked the top of the beat he stopped and, after releasing the treble hook from the butt ring of his 11-foot, hollow-glass, carp-rod, he cast the 3-inch yellow belly and 1-ounce bomb weight diagonally downstream, to land in the water under the far bank. Since he had started fishing four hours earlier the water had risen and coloured perceptibly. Already he had changed from a 2-inch blue and silver wooden devon to the yellow belly.

Half-an-hour later and a hundred yards downstream of the boundary, still with no sign of a fish, thoughts of calling it a day were running through his head. Perhaps just one last cast in the Grayling Pool, a spot where the river widened and deepened below a shallow, weedy run. He held the rod almost vertical as the minnow swung across the tail of the pool and then lowered the tip to within a foot of the water surface and slowly began to reel in. As the retrieve was completed the line slanted down steeply into the water, almost at his feet.

The cast was practically fished out – but could that have been a knock? He lifted the tackle from the water and decided to have another "positively last" cast.

Five last casts later, as the minnow swept round under the near bank the rod plunged into a curve as a fish took firmly, hooked itself and turned away downstream. The long rod bent more steeply and Harry's numb fingers fumbled with the clutch control on his fixed spool reel to ease the pressure slightly. As he began to wake up to the fact that he had, at last, hooked a fish his heart sank as his adversary rose to the surface and thrashed from side to side. He knew at once that it was a kelt.

The battle was brief and a minute or two after the fish was hooked, it was tailed and slid onto the wet, grassy bank where it flexed its body and thumped the muddy ground with its tail. The flanks of the fish were bright, shining silver but on its "cheeks" and gill covers were a few red spots, relics of the spawning livery which it had flaunted only six weeks earlier. He returned it carefully to the water. Characteristically, he was encouraged by the capture of the kelt and fished on for a further hour, only packing in when the wind increased to force ten and he was in danger of being dumped in the swollen river by a sudden, squalling gust of rain-laden air. He had nothing to show for five-and-a-half hours' fishing!

Harry fished for another forty hours, in all, during March of that year and caught a further nine salmon, *all kelts*, which he returned to the water with a variety of emotional comments. In the following year (1983) his reward for a cold, frosty six o'clock start on a spring day, was a solid bite as his home-made blue and silver wooden devon swung across the tail of the Boundary Pool. It was instantly clear that the fish was no kelt as it bored deeply towards the far bank. In the next ten minutes he followed it down through the shallows, where he caught a tantalising glimpse of broad tail and purple-tinged flank, then back upstream into the pool. Eventually it surfaced, wallowing on its side, close under the near bank to be gaffed and slid ashore. Harry unhooked his prize and checked his watch – 7.50 a.m. His broad grin suggested that he thought it was not a bad start to the season. With his confidence boosted he went on to catch three further spring fish before the end of April; the four salmon weighing 18, 16$\frac{1}{2}$, 14 and 21 pounds.

Harry on the bank of the river Frome with a fine salmon caught by spinning.

The attraction of the devon minnow

The captures of the kelts and fresh-run spring fish show not only the range of emotions which can be experienced in salmon fishing but also give some idea of the equipment suitable for catching large, powerful fish in smallish, deep and snaggy rivers. All the fish were taken on that most traditional of salmon spinning lures, the devon minnow. It is no accident that these simple lures are so popular, because their form and construction has evolved largely for the purpose of catching one species. *Salmo salar*, at one stage of its life. This unusually specific approach to angling is worth considering in detail. First, we can examine the reasons for the effectiveness of the devon minnow and the best tackle and design of lure for the job.

The materials of which the devons are made can be taken item by item. First, the central tube may be either plastic (e.g. ballpoint pen refill) or metal. In either case the ends should be smoothly rounded without rough or sharp edges or fragments of hardened glue. A fast spinning lure can quickly damage and weaken the nylon mount (which is in all respects superior to the wire mounts often sold with commercially made minnows). Both metal and plastic tubes are satisfactory, the only difference being in density (weight), which should be borne in mind in relation to the conditions in which it is intended to fish and the volume and buoyancy of the material from which the body of the minnow is made.

Wooden, rubber and plastic devon minnows are all quite suitable for fishing *in the fast flowing water* associated with large spring fish. The ideal is a combination of tube, body, fins, hook and lead which has neutral buoyancy (i.e. no tendency

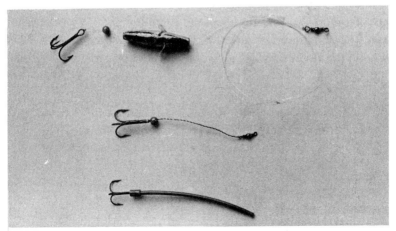

Simple and effective mount for wooden or plastic devon minnows; the lead link can be attached to the front eye of the swivel. This method is definitely superior to the use of the two commercially available mounts shown below.

to either float or sink). In general, the force of the flowing water will compensate to some extent for any deficiencies in this respect. Heavy lures will tend to "hang down" and may snag the river bed in moderate flow; light ones will ride higher than is desirable and will also require more lead to take them down to the river bed. Ideally, the height of the lure above the gravel should be controlled only by varying the length of drop from the swivel to the lead, so neutrally buoyant lures are best.

Having made or purchased more or less streamlined bodies drilled out and lined with plastic or metal tubes it is then necessary to fit fins. The fins can be made of metal, plastic or even rubber. It is possible that the softer materials may confer a slight advantage in the fact that they are less likely to jam in the jaws of a taking fish; however, many good salmon have

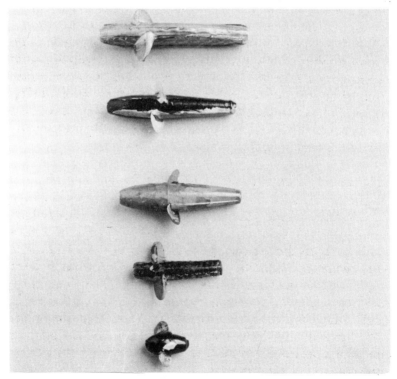

A range of home-made devon minnows. The lures range from $\frac{3}{4}$ to $2\frac{1}{2}$ inches. All have caught salmon.

been caught on devons with metal or hard plastic fins. It would also seem reasonable to make fins as small as possible, crescent-shaped fins being superior to "ear-like" ones in this respect, but it must be remembered that larger and/or more steeply angled fins are required for use where the flow is slower. In general, an angle of about 60° to the long axis of the minnow is a good compromise.

A bearing is needed for the central tube to spin against. Once again it is possible to buy custom-made bearings which fit over the eye of the treble hook, but these are much less effective than simple plastic beads. Although the former are supposed to keep the hook in line with the tube of the minnow, the extra friction is not worth the suggested advantage. A decent half-blood knot is perfectly adequate to keep the hook aligned with the trace. Materials other than soft plastic for beads are not worth considering because of the risk of damage to the trace.

Treble hooks for use with devon minnows should always be of high quality. A few pence is a small price to pay for total assurance in the hook-hold. It is hardly worth repeating that hooks should have a large enough gape to avoid being masked by the lure and should be kept needle sharp. A size 4 round bend treble is a reasonable size for normal, cigar-shaped, $2\frac{1}{2}$-inch to 3-inch devons.

Large or small lure?
On the question of size of these fast-spinning lures we have few constructive suggestions. In general, on the rivers which we have fished, salmon anglers use large devons of, say, 3 inches early in the season when the water is deep and dirty. As it clears and falls they will switch to somewhat smaller lures. The fact that even small grilse will (at least sometimes) take huge chromium or nickel-plated plugs of $3\frac{1}{2}$ inches in length suggests that even the *rules* which dictate the use of large lures in cold water and small lures in the warmer months are far from immutable. It would be interesting to see some controlled experiments.

The psychology of anglers may well account for some of the traditional attitudes to lures (for salmon and for other species) and it can do no harm at all to re-examine the dogma which has built up around our sport. In so far as summer salmon are mainly grilse of only a few pounds in weight and the springers tend to be "submarines", big baits in spring and small ones in summer could well make sense. However, in the rivers which we have fished, the warmer waters of summer do not make it essential to fish with tiny lures or baits.

A salmon of 15 pounds taken in spring on a big spoon.

Frequently the large lures will be coloured in green and yellow halves (yellow bellies) and the smaller ones blue and silver. To obtain a metallic or highly reflective finish the usual paint may be replaced with tinfoil or aluminium foil. (A good gold paper is found on the wrappers of "Caramac" bars and silver paper on many other types of chocolate.) An alternative to chocolate wrapping paper is the commercially produced "flectolite" tape, obtainable in various colours, which catches every glimmer of available light. This said, we have no *evidence* that any one of these colours is better than another. In the chalk rivers of southern England more large spring fish are probably caught on yellow bellies than on any other combination, but this is almost certainly because this is the most popular pattern in the early season. We have seen fish caught on devons painted almost every colour of the rainbow and even on plain brown, wood-finish models which had lost every vestige of colour.

The easy option

Neutrally buoyant devon minnows do have considerable advantages as salmon lures. Some of these they share with other lure types; others are unique.

1 The devon will fish at a distance from the river bed which is fixed by the length of "drop" to the lead.
2 The movement of the flowing water imposes the action and vibration to the lure.
3 The lure attracts by both vibration and flash.
4 When a fish takes, the body of the lure slides up the trace (unless it is stuck on a fancy wire mount). This leaves the fish attached by the hook alone, thus preventing any possibility of the lure being used as a lever to break, straighten or lever out the hooks. This advantage is at least potentially applicable to some other types of lure (e.g. the Kynoch-Killer) and is a function of the sliding tube method of attachment.

To sum up, the wooden, rubber or plastic devon is a cheap, effective and easily fished lure most useful in flowing water. The tendency to cause line twist, which is common to all revolving spinners, is avoided by the standard method of attaching the trace to the lead with an anti-kink dropper. Only a single swivel is required in setting up the tackle.

Wooden devon minnows can easily be made any shape or size. Mike has made up an elongate, sand-eel-shaped devon (6 inch × ½ inch) which he used successfully from a dinghy at sea. By dangling the lure on a conventional rig in strong tidal currents he caught quite a few pollack and pouting. The problem with such a lure is the presence of only a single treble at the tail end. Many large predatory fish take their victims with a side-swipe, gripping them about midway along the body, thus missing out on the hook. Fat, barrel-shaped devons were referred to by the late Colonel Crow as "fat sprats" and were believed (by him) to be particularly attractive to salmon. Again, our experience suggests that they are at least as good as the more streamlined articles.

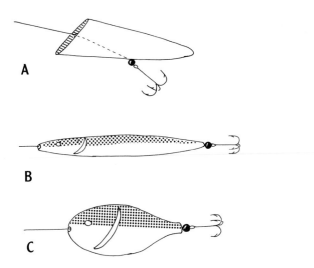

Figure 8
Three lures which slide freely up the line, preventing the fish from
using the lure as a lever. **A** Kynoch type plug. **B** Slim devon
minnow. **C** Fat sprat devon minnow.

As already mentioned, the neutral buoyancy devon minnow is an easy lure to use because, provided it is cast more or
less accurately down and across the river, it will tend to "fish
itself". The rod is simply raised or lowered, allowing the lead
to bump its way across the bottom with the lure sweeping
slowly around in a wide arc and ticking over at a fixed height
above the bed. When the tackle reaches the near bank it is
retrieved slowly. The depth, at this stage, is controlled by
keeping the lead more or less in contact with the bottom until
the line is short enough for the next cast.

Because salmon often lie on the outside of river bends in
deep, fast-flowing water, it is often possible to fish a devon by
what we call dangling. This method also depends on the
tendency for these lures to "fish themselves" in flowing water.
The tackle is lowered under the rod point at the head of the
run and, by repeatedly raising the rod quickly and lowering
back more slowly until the lead touches down, the tackle can
be worked down each swim. A take may come at any stage
and the fish will often hang itself on as it grabs the lure and
turns across the flow, setting the hook in its scissors.

One thing which is worth remembering when it comes to fishing deep bends is that the flow in such places is not a simple curve but a spiral. Salmon, which like most fish prefer to face into the flow, may lie with their heads towards the near bank.

Why do salmon take?
Having pointed out the virtues of the traditional wooden devon minnow we should now consider whether this is in fact the *best* spinner for salmon fishing. Since our quarry is not feeding in freshwater, are there any useful criteria which we can apply to the choice of a lure? The basic assumption is that a fish, fresh in from the tide, will respond best to something that looks like food; possibly a small fish, squid or prawn, a few inches in length. It is noticeable that after being in the river for a few weeks (or longer) fish tend to "lose interest". It seems likely that this staleness and change in feeding behaviour is caused by the onset of breeding condition (development of eggs or milt; depletion of food and energy reserves; change from silver camouflage to spawning colours, and so

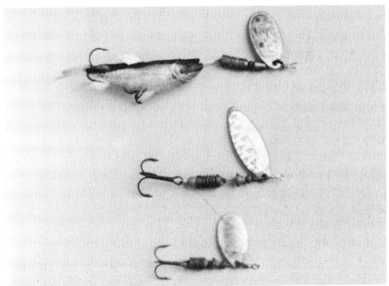

Bar-spoons which can be fished down and across or cast upstream and spun down for salmon and trout.

on). There is precious little that any angler can do about this non-response except to observe that, like most biological changes, it probably progresses more quickly in warm weather. In late summer, towards the end of the salmon fishing season, there is a further change in condition of the fish as the (winter) spawning time draws near. The large male salmon in particular develop aggressive territorial behaviour patterns and will at this time attack almost anything which enters their "patch".

The paternal, protective urges of the cock fish make them vulnerable to the angler, because they will chase and snap at almost anything. At this time it would seem that the larger the lure the better, since the angler is trying to simulate a rival or intruder rather than offer an item of diet. In fact the largest salmon which we have ever seen, a massive fish of well over 50 pounds, was a big, red, male fish which took an 8-inch plug being used for autumn pike. Just take a look at the game fishing magazines for confirmation; almost all the huge salmon illustrated with their smiling captors, at the back end of the year, are clearly prospective fathers which mistook the angler's lure for a rival.

Bar-spoons

To return to the matter of lures, there are quite a few alternatives to the wooden devon. Bar-spoons are very effective salmon attractors; both the simple blade-spinner with a weighted bar and the version with a soft, latex-rubber fish attached at the back end. The Mepps-Mino is the best of the latter type. In using bar-spoons the principle is the same as that which applies to devon minnows. It is better to use a relatively lightweight spoon than a heavy, fast-sinking one. However, the unweighted or lightly weighted shaft will cause excessive line twist and the version with a rubber fish is an excellent compromise.

Bar-spoons can be fished down and across in the conventional fashion, but generally it is more effective to cast upstream or up and across and, by retrieving slightly faster than the flow, keep the blade turning. How can you judge the pace of the current? In fact it is easier than it sounds. Cast; allow the lure to sink to the desired depth; give a jerk with the rod to start the blade turning and, keeping the line taut, reel just fast enough to keep the lure spinning. A little too slow and a decrease in tension on the line tells you that the lure is no longer working. Salmon will frequently chase bar-spoons fished in this way for a long distance and, on taking, will usually turn and hook themselves. A small uptrace weight a yard or so above the lure will sometimes help to keep it down.

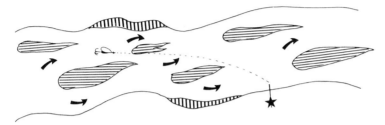

Figure 9
By casting upstream and retrieving just a little faster than the flow, a bar spoon may be made to follow the main current between weed beds.

The versatile plug bait

There has been much controversy about the use of plugs for salmon fishing. In our part of the country (Dorset) these lures have at times been banned for all or part of the season on some rivers. At present the Wessex Water Authority licence states that: "No person shall use ... any ... plug before the 15th of May in any year." Such restrictions are in our view difficult to justify, for plugs are in no sense unsporting and in fact they are the only artificial baits which can be fished most effectively on weightless tackle without swivels, traces or other paraphernalia.

Plug baits vary a good deal in form, ranging from simple curved metal or plastic "bananas" (flatfish, wigglers etc.) to unbelievably fish-like creations shaped and painted to resemble particular bait fish. For salmon fishing there may be little point in trying to fish with a replica of any particular species, although it seems probable that a fresh-run fish would respond best to a replica of the silvery pelagic fish which it ate in its sea-going days (which certainly did not resemble green and yellow wooden cylinders). However, it is true that almost any plug will tempt fish. In our early years of salmon fishing we often used the ABU Hi-Lo, one of the few commercially available plugs with an effective adjustable lip, to allow fishing at different depths. The Hi-Lo is a slow-medium sinker with a rather chunky plastic body and a somewhat sluggish action – probably because it is made of rather dense (heavy) materials. Despite this slow wriggle these plugs caught lots of salmon. Blue ones, green ones, white ones with red heads,

Hi-Lo plugs with lips adjusted for deep (top), midwater (centre), or shallow (bottom) running. Because of their versatility, lures with adjustable lips are good for fishing unknown waters.

even luminous ones, all tempted their fair share of fish.

Using the adjustable Hi-Lo is (and was) perhaps the best introduction to plug fishing which it is possible to have. The principle of the lip (scoop, diving vane) soon becomes clear when you can fold it up or down to order. It is immediately obvious that the action of the lure suffers when the lip is set to give very shallow or very deep diving and that the best wiggle is in the middle range. It is also apparent that salmon (and other fish) will quite often take plugs which do not have much action at all when they are retrieved slowly or held steady in a gentle flow.

Salmon fishing in fast-flowing water, which is often several feet deep, gives scope for using fast-sinking metal plugs and one of the best of these is the Canadian Wiggler which, because it is rather heavy (made of brazed metal pipe), is most effective in strongly flowing water. All that is needed is to cast down and across the flow and, by using the rod, guide the lure through the most likely holding places. If it is known that a fish is in residence it is often possible to manoeuvre the plug to a point just upstream of it and to hold the lure in position, while it wriggles seductively in the current and is taken or rejected.

We have mentioned the ABU Hi-Lo and the Canadian Wiggler as plugs which catch salmon but, in practice, just about any plug will do the job. Some cheap, mass-produced plastic types are pretty good – but a trial is essential to ensure that the hook fixings and nose loop are truly secure. Tried and trusted lures of reputable make such as Rapala or Heddon are generally totally reliable – although Mike once had a tail treble pulled out of a small Heddon plug by a $\frac{3}{4}$-pound trout. The only way to be absolutely certain about your plugs is to make them yourself with strong, all-through wire fixings. But if D.I.Y. lacks appeal, then the Rapala range of balsa-bodied plugs seems to be totally reliable in action, strength and security and they come in all the main variations of floating, sinking and different degrees of dive.

Finally, a few tips about the use of plugs. Normally they are fished with a *small* swivel or clip to allow free movement and easy change. Even the smallest swivels are strong enough for most situations, particularly in view of the fact that plugs should always be fished on the lightest practical line to enhance casting and lure action.

At times it may be useful to fish a buoyant plug, say a J7 or J9 Rapala, with a paternoster style rig which fixes the dis-

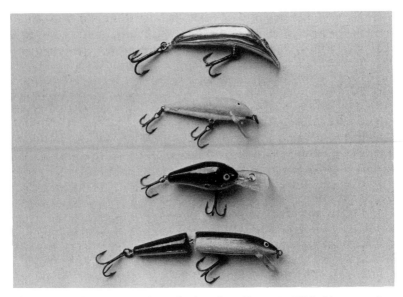

Two sinking plugs (top) and two floating plugs (bottom). With this range of lures the angler is equipped to fish for salmon under all conditions.

tance of the lure from the river bed and allows it to be fished straight up and down or after the fashion of a wooden devon.

Because they are basically chunky, solid, rigid lures, plugs may occasionally lever themselves out of the jaw of a seemingly well-hooked salmon but we have found this to be a fairly infrequent problem. The really fussy angler can fiddle about with break-away hook mounts or sliding body, Kynoch-Killer type plugs but the advantages are marginal. Like barspoons, plugs can be fished either upstream or downstream to good effect.

Success with spoons

One of the most popular salmon attractors is the simple spoon. ABU Toby spoons and other similar lures are widely used (in fact Hugh Falkus reckons that these lures are the best attractors but not the best hookers). The main problem with metal spoons is that of adjusting the weight and size of the spoon needed to the depth and velocity of the water. Too small and light and the spoon skitters across the surface (but may still sometimes catch fish); too heavy and you are straight into the river bed. Traditionally, a salmon lure should be fished as deep as possible without hooking the bottom. If the river bed is uneven, the current is variable or there are lots of weed beds present, perfect control of a simple spoon can be almost a work of art.

In general a wide, flat spoon is easier to control than a narrow one of similar weight because it will sink more slowly. However, only experience and long practice of these lures will give the necessary confidence to use them to the best effect. One excellent method is to lower them to the river bed, in a known lie, and by raising and lowering the rod point to fish them sink and draw, almost like a pirk.

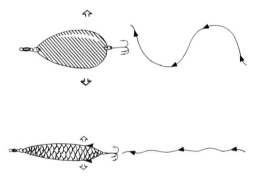

Figure 10
A wide, flat spoon with a slow sweeping action is easier to control than a narrow one of the same weight.

Despite their drawbacks spoons are first-class salmon lures. Howard Leatham, one of our pals, never fished with anything but a Toby in the early part of the season. His best catch was two fresh run springers in half-an-hour. For anyone who has the same faith as Howard we can only say "stick to your spoons". Plenty of information on their use and effectiveness can be found in the pages of many good books on salmon fishing.

CHAPTER ELEVEN

PART-TIME PREDATORS AND BAITED LURES

Select your species

Having written about the advantages of spinning which arise out of the freedom from bait-buying or collecting, it may seem strange to suggest that the addition of natural bait to artificial lures could improve catches. However, John Garrad in his book, *Sea Angling with the Baited Spoon*, showed that a spoon garnished with bait can tempt some surprising catches. Two important points were revealed by Garrad's experiments in the Hamble estuary; first, differences in presentation of the spoon were important, so that trolled spoons only caught flounders and drifted spoons only caught eels; second, the type of bait used did not seem to matter very much. The last point is pretty fundamental since, as most anglers are well aware, both eels and flounders can be *very* fussy about baits fished on normal tackle.

Garrad fished only for flounders, eels and school bass but he mentioned quite a few accidental catches to anglers using his methods; wrasse, pouting, plaice, dabs and so on. Perhaps the first real addition to his exciting discoveries came from another south-coast estuary at Christchurch. Anglers fishing in Christchurch harbour discovered that the attachment of an inch or two of worm to a small bar-spoon resulted in amazing catches of grey mullet. The mullet, mostly fresh-water-loving thin-lips, seemed to find the combination of spinning blade and ragworm attractive and impressive catches were reported by devotees of the method. Curiously, their enthusiasm has not really spread to other areas.

On our own stretch of the Dorset coast thick-lipped mullet are frequently taken by anglers using a variety of conventional methods and baits. Having been convinced of the "Christchurch story" by one of our pals, Steve Pitts, we decided to try out the baited spoon for the local thick-lips. Steve gave us a few of his secret weapons; ultra-light "Jenspoon" barspoons with the shafts adorned with red plastic beads. The entire structure is so light that it is quite unsuitable for normal spinning because the blade, the bar and the hooks all turn actively together and cause horrendous line twist. The addition of a strip of bait to the treble hook damps down this rotation and adds a little casting-weight to the lure.

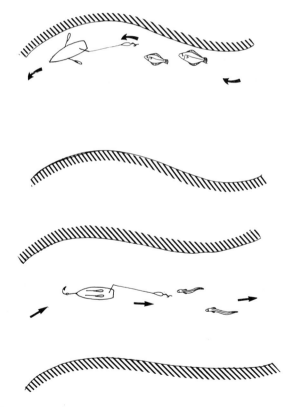

Figure 11
Baited "flounder" spoon trolled with the current to catch flounders or drifted from an anchored boat for eels.

*A thick-lipped mullet of 3 pounds 8 ounces which was caught on a
ragworm-baited "Jenspoon" spun from the shore.*

Tempting a thick lip

The best way to describe the method of fishing with these
spoons is probably to give an account of Mike's own experiments. Steve Pitts had told him the basics – "When you feel
a bite, just keep reeling, etc. etc." – and had regaled him with
tales of large bags of smallish fish; "one-a-cast" is a phrase
which springs to mind.

Armed with information from the experts Mike drove
down to the shore on a spring tide in September. Very few
mullet were showing in the sheltered corner which he had
chosen to fish so he was not tempted to set up the fly rod. His
tackle was an 11-foot, through-actioned, carbon carp-rod
and a Mitchell fixed spool reel loaded with 6-pound line. The
"Jenspoon" was clipped on to a tiny link-swivel and three
inches of ragworm was suspended from the treble hook. He
swung the lure out and, lifting the rod tip, watched the silver
blade flutter along just beneath the surface.

He stood by the edge of the calm sea and cast the lure five
or six yards out from the margin. After allowing the spoon
and worm to sink for a second or so he began a slow retrieve
with the rod point a few inches above the water. There was of
course no response, and a further dozen or more casts met
with the same result. Then a couple of mullet swirled, close in

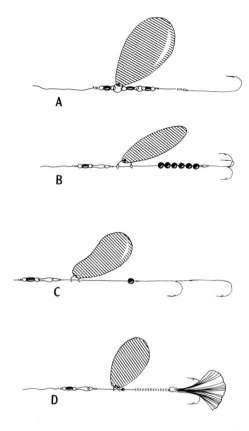

Figure 12
Four types of spoon used for "non-predatory" fish. **A** Flounder spoon.
B Mullet spoon. **C** Gurnard spoon. **D** Roach spoon.
A, B and C are normally baited with ragworm or other baits.

and some distance to his left. He swung the rod again and the
spoon plopped into the sea, beyond the fish and about a yard
out from the beach.

As the slow retrieve started he felt something gently plucking at the bait. He continued to wind steadily and the plucking persisted almost until the lure finally emerged from the
water and swung freely from the tip ring. The plucking was
repeated on the following cast and, intermittently, on several
of the next half-dozen.

By now several thoughts were running through Mike's mind. The bites (he was sure they *were* bites) must be mullet. Why had he not made contact? Despite what he had been advised he had even tried a couple of sharp strikes without the slightest hint of a fish. Was the section of worm the right size? The first fish, on any unfamiliar method, is always the most difficult. Pushing the loss of confidence to the back of his mind Mike continued to fish in the same way as before. At least he was getting bites and it is never wise to change tactics without giving each method a decent trial.

Half-an-hour and innumerable plucks later despair was beginning to set in but, just as a change of tackle was imminent, success! A bite developed at the first few turns of the reel and the culprit seemed very determined. As the lure approached Mike's feet he could just see the grey shape of a following mullet sucking and plucking at the trailing worm. The slight swell was swirling around a prominent rock which stood just clear of the water and, when the spoon and its follower entered the swirl, there was a sudden heavy pull and Mike found himself firmly attached to a hard-fighting mullet. The fish tore about violently and, in the way of mullet, refused to give up but eventually it was netted and weighed in at $3\frac{1}{2}$ pounds.

Despite Mike's persistence there was only one further event in the session. Several additional bites occurred and they were, to all intents, identical. However, shortly after the capture of the thick-lip, as the lure was lifted from the sea, a second fish – a 6-inch sand-smelt – hooked itself. As already mentioned, the bites of the two species were indistinguishable despite the great difference in size and fighting capabilities (the little sand-smelt was swung "to hand" like a tiny roach or dace).

So three more species can be added to Garrad's list; thin- and thick-lipped mullet and sand-smelt. (He did in fact report a single mullet caught on a 3-inch flounder spoon.) The significant thing is that while fish such as mullet, eels and flounders can be caught in large numbers on *baited* lures (numbers often far in excess of the results from conventional bait fishing) few, if any, would be taken in many hours of spinning with *unbaited* lures.

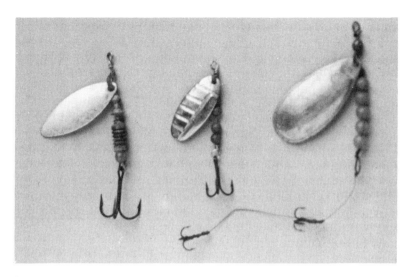

Lightweight spoons. The spoon on the left is a conventional metal-bodied Mepps and would not be as good for use with bait as the other two spoons.

Some other spoon-fed fish

On charter trips Harry has used a large baited spoon to outfish other anglers after plaice – nothing unusual about that perhaps – but in the course of catching the plaice he also took red gurnard on the worm-baited spoon. In fact this recalls the use of a baited (kidney-shaped) bar-spoon by Dr Michael Kennedy specifically for catching gurnard (grey ones in this case). Although Dr Kennedy gives no details of the method in his book *The Sea Angler's Fishes* he does comment that the eleven fish illustrated were taken "from the shore". Match anglers (and others) interested in big bags of fish from the shore could certainly do worse than experiment with baited spoon tactics.

One other point of interest which relates to the use of baited lures was suggested to us by our friend, Dave Cooling. In recent years Dave has done quite a bit of deep sea wreck-fishing. Much of this fishing is for large predatory fish and involves various methods of presenting artificial lures, pirks, muppets, redgills and so on. Dave says that these methods may be just as selective as the flounder and mullet tactics described earlier. A simple unbaited pirk tends to catch cod;

the addition of mackerel strip to a similar lure will result in the capture of ling; and a rubber eel on a long trace over the same wreck may attract pollack and coalfish. Here are the seeds of more experiment and improvement.

The addition of bait to a spinner is not simply a matter of hedging-your-bets against failure of one or the other approach. It is a *totally different* way of fishing, enabling you to make good catches of worthwhile fish when other methods might fail or, at best, be far inferior. American anglers are absolute fanatics for adorning their lures with rubber worms, feathers, rubber squids, lumps of pork rind and so on. Our transatlantic cousins obviously think that these additions are worthwhile; clearly they are obtaining good results but we have yet to see (despite much reading) a reasoned explanation as to why any of these additives should be more attractive than the others.

Schooled to take a lure

Before considering how to extend the possibilities of baited lure fishing it is worth considering *why* fish like mullet should take a lure at all. These fish normally feed on algae or other tiny particles and, although they will occasionally nip at a plug or spoon, they normally decline to bite. Mullet are, first and foremost, schooling fish with a very strong group instinct. The presence of a feeding mullet has been shown to stimulate feeding activity in every other fish in sight.

In many schooling species, when one fish in a shoal has found an item of food (e.g. a worm) all the others want a share and chase after the lucky finder in an effort to pinch its prize. Possibly the baited bar-spoon looks like a smaller fish carrying a desirable morsel and the mullet try to make it give up its prey by bullying it. In the same way, in the bird world, sea birds like skuas and herring gulls will obtain much of their food by pestering and robbing weaker species. If this idea is correct, most schooling fish should be susceptible to the attractions of a baited spoon.

To widen the field a little we recall that Richard Walker, in his book *Still Water Angling*, illustrated some very large roach (possibly roach hybrids?) which had been caught on lightweight bar-spoons armed with small trebles, set well to the rear and decorated with feathers. Apparently the fish were susceptible to these feather-baited spoons in the early part of the season. One cannot fail to be struck by the similarity between these roach-fishing tactics and the mullet spinning methods already described. It seems certain that the principle is the same in both cases. An angler with initiative, patience and access to waters where shoaling roach or other fish of the carp family grow to a good size, could possibly produce spectacular catches by developing his own mini, *lightweight*, long-shanked worm or maggot/baited bar-spoons. The technique will probably involve a longish rod for lure control, lines of 3-6 pounds B.S. on a fixed spool reel and a very slow retrieve. The approach will be suck-it-and-see. This seems, to us, to be one of the most exciting challenges which remain in angling, for while we have personally caught such unlikely species as dace, rudd and bream on small, unbaited bar-spoons, Heaven knows what we might have caught if we had had the foresight to add bait to the hooks. Here indeed, is scope for research.

A chub of 4 pounds 8 ounces caught on a small bar-spoon. Large chub often include small fish in their diet.

Part-time predators

Other part-time predators are much more susceptible to lures than the above species. Chub, barbel and grayling are quite often caught on unbaited lures being used for other fish. We have both landed respectable barbel on wooden devons intended for salmon and the capture in years past of barbel up to record size (14-pound plus) by salmon anglers is common knowledge. The barbel with its undershot, whiskery mouth, does not look like any sort of a predator but the chub, in contrast, is rather like a living coal-scuttle, prepared to eat almost anything. We have caught a great many chub, of all sizes, on conventional baits and tackle. We have also caught quite a few on small spoons, bar-spoons and spinners when we used, regularly, to fish the Dorset Stour. More recently, Mike had a letter from a friend, Bob Spurgeon, who has taken things a bit further. We quote from Bob's letter:

As you are interested in spinning (for coarse fish) in fresh water I will expand a little more on my experiences. I have been fishing in the Bath area now for over twenty years and over these years I have tried many different approaches, by nature I tend to pick a method and fully explore its potential for a whole season. This year I was determined to give plugs a try.

I have been using small spinners (bar-spoons) for years, usually presented without a trace on four-pound line, fixed spool reel and 10ft Mk IV (fibreglass) rod . . . In my early days I regularly caught perch (to one-and-a-half-pounds) and chub (of similar size) using this gear, but some of the chub were quite small.

Last year, when I returned to lure fishing, it was specifically to try plugs and not spoons or spinners. The first thing I had to do was to find if they would catch anything at all and so, in early April, I fished a Rapala 5 GFR downstream in very blustery weather and, on the retrieve, took my first plug-caught trout, a rainbow (the first of many on that lure) . . .

Now a few notes on the species – *chub* – I'll put these first as they are my main quarry at the moment. The plug is definitely *selective of the larger fish* and not, I think, purely as a predatory thing (I find that most of my live minnows end up being scoffed by fish of about half-a-pound; it is *rare* to take one that small on the plug). Most chub strike the plug almost immediately, I guess it needs to intrude on their territory suddenly to be effective. That is not to say that they will not turn and follow it for a while, but a steadily retrieved plug pulled across the shoal is *no good*, it needs to be splashed in amongst them. Many takes are almost instantaneous. Bearing this in mind I feel that pattern and colouration are not important.

Perch – There are no large perch left in my river, following their disappearance several years ago, but there are quite a few smaller ones. These little fish (up to half-a-pound but biggest at one-pound) always engulf the plug from behind. They are not very good at it and a steady retrieve is required for them to be successful.

A grayling of 1 pound 10 ounces caught on a bar-spoon. Such lures are often selective for larger specimens.

Grayling, like chub, will readily take spinning lures. In rivers up around the Arctic Circle the use of spinners is a standard method of catching these fish. Chalkstream grayling are no different from their northern relatives and a Mepps-type bar-spoon fished slowly down and across will often attract a large specimen. In this respect the spinning lure again selects for the better fish.

It should, by now, be obvious that the capture of large coarse fish on plugs, spoons and spinners is no accident and that anglers with the approach and application shown by Bob Spurgeon are on the verge of a considerable break-through in techniques. "Why," you may ask, "have spinning tactics not been developed already if they have so much potential?" We gave the answer in Chapter 2, but it is worth repeating: by tradition, many British anglers have no faith in artificial lures, baited or unbaited. Only when enough anglers devote sufficient effort to developing these methods will they begin to appreciate their possibilities.

CHAPTER TWELVE

PERCH, TROUT AND SEA TROUT

Throwing some light on perch

Any account of spinning in Britain must consider that superb, black-striped hunter, the perch. Almost every coarse angler must have caught small perch but how many consistently take decent specimens? Richard Walker was one of a small group of anglers who took a succession of gigantic perch from Arlesey lake. The fish were caught in deep water on bright winter days and Walker placed a lot of emphasis on light as a major factor governing the exciting sport of perch fishing.

However, perch *will* feed well even when light penetration is less than ideal. Mike recalls that when he was thirteen years old he used to fish, with one of his pals, in a derelict limestone quarry. One evening they were standing on a narrow ledge just above the water surface with the rock face in front of them falling sheer into thirty feet of water. The keep-net, tied firmly to a tough bramble bush, was hanging over the ledge and contained a respectable number of roach of between two and four ounces in weight. Darkness was closing in and they were on the verge of packing up when they heard a strange noise; it sounded like someone smacking the water with an upturned tea spoon. On investigating they found that the cause of the disturbance was the two largest perch they had ever seen. The fish were chopping at the little roach imprisoned in the keep-net.

Hurriedly Mike searched the tackle bag for a decent-sized hook. The only one he could find was the treble which was attached to a large red and white plastic mackerel spinner.

Feverishly the spinner was tied to the 2-pound line, in place
of the light float gear, and a small roach was sneaked out of
the net and lip-hooked on one point of the treble.

As soon as the roach hit the water it was engulfed by the
smaller of the two perch. Mike allowed it to run off for a
couple of yards and then tightened into it, fully conscious of
the crude hooks and delicate line. After a brief but splashy
struggle the fish was netted and lifted out. It weighed 3½
pounds, the biggest Mike had ever caught. Meanwhile its
escort had departed at some speed.

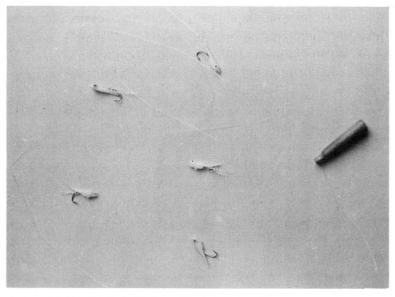

*An unusual rig of "plastic flies" used in Switzerland for catching perch in deep
lakes. The weight shown is about one ounce.*

The two lads grabbed the gear, popped the perch into the
haversack and set off for home to show their parents the fine
catch. But as Mike scrambled up the steep, stony slope the
fish twitched a couple of times inside the canvas bag. He
stopped, took off the bag and opened it. The two boys, almost
awestruck, peered into the folds and a huge, glistening yellow
eye seemed to stare back at them. Overcome with remorse
they hurriedly slid down to the water's edge, slipped the fish
back into the quarry and watched it swim gracefully away.

On the following evening they were down at the same spot again but this time they were fully prepared. Sure enough, as the sun went down the larger of the two perch appeared; once again it began chomping at the small fish in the net. As soon as the bait was lowered into the water it was taken without hesitation, but in his over-eagerness Mike's pal struck too soon and the fish was missed.

On the question of how light affects perch fishing, studies in Sweden have explored the activity patterns of these fish under experimental conditions. Perch were caught in cage traps, transferred to tanks and kept in natural daylight. The activity of the fish was recorded by red (invisible?) light beams and photo cells. This work was carried out to the north of the Arctic Circle. In the cold conditions the perch were only active from June to August, when water temperatures reached $8°-12°$ centigrade. The first thing to note is that

1 *the longer the period of daylight, the more prolonged was the fish activity;*

2 near surface swimming and feeding was *much* greater in the warm months of the year.

3 In June the fish fed only in the middle of the day but in July and August *dawn and dusk* were the peak times.

This double-peak of activity shown by perch, as light intensity changes, is common in many other predatory fish. It seems to be an attempt by the crafty predators to take advantage of the semi-darkness to catch prey unawares *while they are still visible.* Or, in other words, to see without being seen too easily. Sight feeders like perch are able to catch confused prey which are moving from resting to feeding stations, or *vice versa* (i.e. on or off the "night shift").

All these facts agree with the observations of Richard Walker and those of Mike's youth. To put it in a nutshell, perch are mainly active in the hours of daylight but, in the warmer summer months, they feed best at dawn and dusk. Added to this, they will feed at any time when there is an abundance of easy food or when coloured water produces the effect of an artificial dawn or dusk. This was clearly shown by the enthusiasm with which they took our Mepps-Minos when we fished on the River Wylye near Salisbury.

Harry's biggest perch (3 pounds 7 ounces) was caught in August from the River Avon at Stratford. Once again it took just as the light was failing and he was spinning with the only lure he possessed at that time, a small, gold Mepps bar-spoon. In this case his main problem was bringing the fish ashore as it was very lightly hooked and, due to inexperience, Harry was without a net. Like many anglers before and since, he was rescued by a nearby fellow-fisherman.

Perch pack

So, how do perch catch their food? Again, one of Mike's early experiences illustrates the main tactic of the species. He was working his way around the reedy margin of the same quarry from which he caught his first big perch, casting out and retrieving a small buoyant plug. Every gap and hole in the thick feathery beds of milfoil was searched with care but, after two hours of combing the water, there was still no sign of a fish. Suddenly, twenty yards off and well out into the lake, the calm surface of the water was disturbed by dozens of tiny splashes as a shoal of fry sprayed in every direction. Mike watched the spot for a couple of minutes, during which time the "flash expansion" of little fish was repeated three times. Slowly he retraced his steps along the shore until with a long cast the small plug was placed just beyond the disturbed area.

Almost before the line tightened there was a heart-stopping pull and a perch of just under 2 pounds, firmly hooked on the tail treble, was played to the net. Before it became too dark to fish effectively three more big perch and a 7-pound pike (which lunged from a weed bed on the last cast) were landed from the same area.

Once again the sport came at dusk. The sort of action described involved three types of fish living in still water. The prey (rudd) and two types of predator; the perch, a schooling, chasing hunter and the pike, a lurking ambushing form. The way in which such fish interact has been studied by a Canadian researcher named Nursall.

Instead of rudd the Canadian lake held huge schools of fish called spot tail shiners but the predators, perch and pike, were the same. Like rudd, the shiners are small, metallic, surface- or near-surface feeders with mirror-like scales. The shiners even behave like rudd, swimming within a foot or two of the surface with the smaller fish nearest the top and the largest ones deeper down. The fish in a shoal twist and turn in formation, often hesitating and suddenly changing direction. Any attack by a predator results in flash expansion of the shiners with the little fish scattering in all directions from the point of attack. In escaping they often "spray" from the surface of the water, giving away the position of the larger fish. The black spot in front of the shiner's tail fin is a signal to its shoal mates (like the white tails of rabbits) and enables them to react quickly to danger.

From a young age perch swim about in schools and the young fish in a school will often stream along in the same direction, rather like iron filings in a magnetic field. The big adult fish also stream in this way but, in this case, the streaming is usually a form of "pack hunting". Pack hunting gives the perch a better chance of making a capture than they would have on their own. When one perch tires of the chase another member of the pack takes over – rather like hunting dogs after a tiring quarry. A shiner rushing from the attack of one perch may flee into the jaws of another.

Pike also feed on shiners but they do not, as a rule, work in packs. They are solitary predators which take up a totally different approach, lurking in cover until the shiners swim close before sculling around with their paddle-like fins to line up their sights on the target. The tail, dorsal and ventral fins are bent round to one side, setting the "spring" to prepare for launching the body. Ultimately the pike darts at its prey with high efficiency and this form of hunting has been called axial-tracking and lunging.

From the angler's point of view one of the most interesting features is the way in which the feeding activity of one perch attracts the attention of others in the area. This attraction quickly leads to streaming and pack hunting behaviour. Hence, the use of the big flasher-spoons and similar attractors is likely to lead to greatly increased catches of perch and may be an excellent substitute for ground baiting.

Shoal suicide

Because of their sociable nature and the way in which members of a school must compete with their fellows for food, perch are liable to bite very freely. This well known, bold biting habit of "old stripey" often results in big catches over short periods of time. We can both recall catching virtually a fish every cast on several occasions. From small tree-lined ponds, from chalk-river backwaters, from loughs and from canals, we have landed fish after fish by spinning. Depending on the nature of the water the fish have varied in size. From the clear and impoverished waters of the great whin sill in north-east England the average weight of the perch may be only a few ounces (with the pike not much bigger); while from the rich southern rivers every fish in a shoal may be well over a pound.

Because perch tend to feed mostly on smallish fish, little lures are usually effective and the best are those which have the rapid flicker of small fry but can be fished in a controlled fashion near weeds and snags. Bar-spoons fill the bill well and we favour Mepps, or better still Mepps-Mino, which is more controllable and on which most of our larger bags have been taken.

Figure 13
Mepps-Mino, an easily controlled and very effective bar spoon combination.

One last remembered experience may help to emphasise what we have said.

Harry was working in Scotland and, as always, had taken his spinning rod. Having consulted mine host at the local hostelry he discovered that it was possible to fish the club water on the nearby river for two pounds a day (including salmon and sea trout). The following morning he obtained his permit and, after work, he rushed through his dinner and hurried to the river. There were lots of salmon in the stretch

– he could see them – waiting below the fish-ladder of the local power station. Harry decided to make certain that he covered every fish, as he was certain that most of them would already have seen many lures and found them wanting. He began to fish and had only covered about ten yards of bank when the rod jerked slightly. A bite! He struck and the fish was on – a 1-pound perch. The action was repeated about ten times in half a mile of river. Each perch weighed between eight ounces and a pound and all the fish were caught on a Mepps-Mino. Eventually the lure was exchanged for a large Toby spoon and the bites ceased until darkness fell, when the Toby was taken by a 3½-pound sea trout.

A sea trout of 7 pounds 8 ounces which took a plastic "yellow belly" devon minnow intended for salmon.

Spectacular sea trout

We have caught quite a few sea trout over the years, although we would not claim to be in the same league as Hugh Falkus. Anyone with aspirations to catch large numbers of these fish should certainly read his excellent book on the subject. Our main claim to fame with this species is recorded (anonymously) in the Avon and Dorset (now Wessex) Water Authority salmon and sea trout returns for the little River Piddle. The annual catch of sea trout for the river, which we fished for a single season, one day a week on the tidal stretch, showed a more than four-fold increase over the catch for the preceding year. The boost in results was due almost entirely to our efforts with small Mepps bar-spoons fished upstream at dawn or dusk. In fact this was our first and only *real* foray into sea trout fishing and, due largely to our inexperience, we lost several of the bigger fish hooked while spinning (notably one monster hooked on a plug by Mike).

These catches were made despite the rather crude tackle which we were using at the time (the stretch of river was unbelievably snaggy and, with the ever-present possibility of a large salmon, we tended towards the use of heavy lines and hefty rods).

Mike's previous experience of sea trout was gained while he was working for his Ph.D. at Budle Bay on the north-east coast of England. Budle Bay is a large inlet flanked by rolling sand dunes and paved with a wide expanse of fine sand. The grey waters of the North Sea retreat from the flats with each ebbing tide, to reveal twin streams of fresh water wandering across the bay from the inland corners. In the deeper channel formed at the confluence of the two streams Mike spent many hours legering with ragworm for the fat flounders waiting for the return of the tide. His tackle consisted of a trout spinning rod, a small fixed-spool reel and 6-pound line terminating in light leger tackle and a number 6 or 8 eyed hook.

Most of his fishing was done at the crack of dawn before he began his work. Often, as he waited at first light for a "flatty" to take his bait, the quiet would be broken by the loud splash of a leaping fish. This was Mike's first encounter with sea trout and sometimes he would have a clear view of the silver-shining, thick-set body of the fish; arched for an instant above the calm water before it flopped back to send a succession of circling ripples over the surface. As he soon discovered, the sea trout were not interested in ragworm and, perhaps surprisingly, he never contacted one on the legered sand eel which he sometimes used for flounders.

At that time Mike was living with a shepherd, Bob

Edmondson and his family, on a farm close to the village of Belford. He was able to fish the two little streams, the Ross Low and the Waren Burn, which ran into Budle Bay. Eels, flounders and small brown trout were the usual catches but after heavy rain massive brownies would appear like magic in the thick brown water and could be extracted without difficulty on lobworm-baited tackle.

Where the big trout were at other times he never discovered though he tried everything to catch them; bread, worms, flies, minnows, spoons – the lot! One evening after work he decided to spend yet another couple of hours after the elusive monster brown trout. The tackle was the same as that used for the flounders but the business end consisted of a tiny link swivel and a size 1 silver Mepps. He caught a series of $\frac{1}{2}$-pound trout with almost monotonous regularity and, just as the light was failing, he was considering packing in. With the indecision common to most anglers in this situation, he changed his mind and decided to have a couple more casts into the slightly deeper, peaty-looking water under a small footbridge.

On the first cast he let the spinner sink for a couple of seconds and then began to retrieve smartly to keep the blade working as the lure moved with the current. Almost at once there was a heavy pull on the rod top and, to his astonishment, the water exploded as a fish much larger than any he had previously caught launched itself from the water. Five minutes of head-shaking, racing, twisting and thrashing later, he netted a $3\frac{3}{4}$-pound sea trout, beautifully silver but with a rather large head and lean body – despite the fact that it was late June, long after the spawning time.

On reflection, Mike was lucky to land that first fish but since then he has taken many more and still regards them as the most difficult fish to subdue and land, chiefly because of their incredible vitality.

Most of the sea trout which we have caught were taken from rivers and streams but one or two were hooked in their real feeding habitat – the sea. Whilst fishing from the steep rocky cliffs of the Donegal coast in north-west Ireland the Toby spoon, intended for the bronzed and aggressive pollack, would occasionally be taken by a little silver lightning-bolt of a sea-run trout.

As must be obvious, our experience of sea trout in the sea is very limited, but we know that many game fishermen must, like the trout themselves, hanker after the salt tide flooding over the wrack beds of a distant sea loch. There can be few satisfactions greater than the pull of a wild leaping fish hooked on light tackle in the open sea.

Perhaps it may help to bring this dream a little nearer to reality if we recall the scientific observations of Dr Pemberton in some sea lochs of North Argyll. Pemberton netted every two weeks throughout the year to find out more about the movements of the fish after they came down to the sea as smolts. This downstream migration of the little silver fish was usually in mid-May, except in one very dry season when they were delayed by about a month. These "post-smolts". as they were called, passed straight through the loch. On several occasions over four hundred of the small trout were taken in a single haul of the net.

The post-smolts grew very quickly and reached the "whit-ling" stage before returning to the lochs in August and September when they were 8–10 inches in length. About one fish in ten at this time of the year was over 11 inches from nose to

A sea trout weighing 14 pounds 8 ounces caught on a No. 3 Mepps bar-spoon by Jon Bass. A salmon of 10 pounds was taken on the same lure shortly afterwards.

tail. In October and November there were still plenty of whitling about in the lochs but these were augmented by a second run of smolts from the rivers. In the period from December to March whitling were most numerous at the river mouths and just outside the lochs.

In winter about one fish in seven was a skinny, drab-coloured kelt, but in February and March a quarter of the fish were large whitling in the 10-inch bracket and these grew steadily bigger throughout the following spring.

From the angling point of view, at least in Scotland, sea trout could hardly be more obliging. They almost invariably live within 200 yards of the sea's edge and often they are very much closer in; they are very rarely caught at any great distance from the rocks and beaches. Most of the fish caught by anglers were landed in the period from March to May or in late summer and autumn.

From March to November we have spent thousands of rod-hours spinning on the Dorset coast where several of the inflowing rivers are known to have runs of sea trout, yet only rarely have we seen anyone catch one of these fish. Why should this be? We have been unable to find any information on the movements of sea trout in the open sea in this area.

Sampling off the beaches of Scotland throughout the day and night produced peak catches in the nets at sunrise and sunset and *particularly at low tide*. Even allowing for some fish avoiding nets during the daylight hours these results are probably realistic because the fish were seen to move in and out of the river mouths with the tide.

In the open sea the catches of whitling were low in winter when the mature trout averaged 13–14 inches in length and the fish ran up the rivers to spawn from mid-October to mid-November. A recent study on the River Esk showed that many of the whitling wandered to and fro between fresh and salt water several times in the same year.

When they were in the sea lochs the trout were, as we have said, feeding close inshore, often in very shallow water and there they took three main types of food:

1 *fish* which were essentially near-surface swimmers such as sand eels, sprats and herrings;

2 *beach fleas* and *worms* picked up from near the sea bed; and

3 *insects* trapped in the surface film of the salt water.

Young fish and surface insects were eaten mostly in the warmer months of the year and bottom-living animals chiefly in the winter, but the larger fish of more than 8 inches in length fed mainly on fish at all times.

So there we have it – the picture of an almost perfect angler's fish. Hard fighting, spectacularly leaping, living most of its life within easy casting distance of the shore in the shallow margins of the sea, and feeding on surface, mid-water and bottom-living food. This must make the sea trout susceptible to a wide range of angling methods including bottom fishing, float fishing, fly fishing and especially spinning.

Fresh water trout

Biologically, brown trout belong to the same species as sea trout but their feeding grounds are in fresh water and consequently they are generally easier to catch in rivers and lakes than their sea-going counterparts. Brownies (and the alien rainbows) feed to a large extent on small fish, at times when these are abundant. The larger the trout the more often it will fancy a meal of fish. The main problem for the would-be trout spinner is not the fish themselves, but the prejudice which may prevent him or her finding a place to fish.

We have been fortunate in being able to catch trout from a wide variety of waters, using both fly and spinning tackle, and there is no doubt in our minds that each method has its place. In using anything but the very lightest lures (e.g. flies), a fixed spool reel and a spinning rod has *all* the advantages.

As in any form of angling the line strength, and of course the rod, can be matched to the conditions and size of fish to be expected. Normally we would use 3- or 4-pound breaking strain for trout spinning. Note that this is lighter than the cast strength often used by many fly fishermen, particularly when fishing with modern lures.

As usual, a few examples reveal everything. In the introduction to this book we mention an impromptu ("out of season") trip to a chalk stream on which we caught large trout of between 2 and 5 pounds in weight on biggish spinners. In the previous two seasons the largest fish caught on fly by the regular fly-fishermen (according to the club record books) was just $2\frac{3}{4}$ pounds. Now, however good we may be at spinning – and we make no claim to be more than well practised – this is a remarkable difference. It is almost certainly due to the effectiveness of large spinners (Mepps–Minos) for catching big trout (which were obviously feeding largely on a diet of fish).

On another occasion we were on a business trip to the headquarters of our employers, the F.B.A., The Ferry House on Lake Windermere. As usual we took our rods and lure boxes with us and had arranged for one of our pals to buy a couple of licences so that we could fish during our brief stay. After the evening meal we had to attend a function for a number of eminent scientists and local dignitaries. After a couple of hours of small talk, cheese and wine we slipped out, grabbed the rods and made for the nearest water, which happened to be the deep drop-off alongside the ferry landing. Mike tied on a small plug and Harry used a size three Mepps–Mino. We both had trout in mind and our level of excitement was increased when we heard the loud splash of a leaping fish out in the darkness.

The night was pretty black but the sloping stone ramp on which we stood was illuminated by a large street lamp. Mike chose to fish in the semi-circle of light and was soon into a fish – a small jack pike. As he played it to hand Harry continued to fling his bar-spoon out into the darkness. Suddenly there was a mighty disturbance away to his left and, at the same instant, his rod crashed round into a steep curve. The ensuing battle was fast and furious but neither of us knew what was going on until a big brown trout appeared under the glow of the lamp. We soon had the fish ashore: it weighed $5\frac{3}{4}$ pounds.

Despite a further hour of spinning there were no more bites so we packed up the tackle and made our way back to say our polite goodbyes to the V.I.Ps. The late Doctor Winifred Frost – a famous ichthyologist and fanatical trout angler (co-author with Dr Brown of that excellent book, *The Trout*) – had noticed our absence and, shrewdly guessing the reason

for our disappearance, asked whether we had caught anything. Harry produced his prize and held it out for inspection. Dr Frost was clearly impressed and enquired what fly
the fish had taken. The "fly" was duly presented, to be
greeted by a loud gasp of horror; clearly it was implied that
no self-respecting trout should be silly enough to ingest such
a monstrosity!

By no means all our trout have been caught at dusk or in
dirty water, in fact most of our trout fishing is done in very clear
streams. By casting upstream and retrieving with the flow
even the wiliest chalk-stream or moorland beck trout can be
induced to take a spinning lure. At times trout, like most fish,
will refuse to bite whatever is offered. On such occasions it is
worth trying to offer live baits (minnows, loach or bullheads)
after dark. However, if an artificial is *very* realistic it may be
taken even during a period of low, warm water. The places
to fish are where there is a lively flow such as rapids, weirpools
and mill races. In fact Mike once made a plug from balsa
which was coloured and painted like a 2-inch minnow (grey
back, silver belly, black stripe and all). His first ever cast with
the lure ("just to try it out") was into the race-way below a
wooden hatch on a small chalk stream. The plug was held
back against the flow but, because of the turbulent white
water, it refused to submerge. As the model minnow bounced
about on the foaming, rushing current a $3\frac{1}{4}$-pound brown
trout launched itself like a Polaris missile and, seizing the
plug, was firmly hooked. It was landed after a fierce struggle
in the confines of the small pool and on that successful note we
end our book – but with a postscript.

We do not, of course, advocate breaking rules and regula-
tions but it is worth noting that, in many cases, the rules are
designed to make catching fish more difficult. This may, in
fact, be necessary to protect the stock from unscrupulous or
greedy anglers. Nowadays, in the age of commercially run
put-and-take fisheries, the owners will often make a great
many rules, chiefly to obtain the best financial gain from their
investment. It would be (and is) a pity if such rules of
convenience were to become water authority byelaws, thus
restricting all anglers and stifling initiative and new ideas.

Angling is faced with enough problems from pollution, indiscriminate netting or commercial overfishing (including immature fish in the case of species such as bass) and the anti-angling lobby, without having artificial divisions within our sport.

Is there any simple method of choosing a good (effective) lure? We will try to set down a brief account of our own approach.

The first thing to consider is the probable food of your quarry – and the *shape* of that food. Is it chunky like a roach, crayfish or wrasse? Is it slim and wriggly like a leech, eel, lamprey or rockling or is it somewhere in between like a squid, dace, minnow or mackerel? In the first case you might select a fat-devon, a broad wobbling spoon, a wide-bladed Mepps, a Fat-Rap or Big S plug or a Canadian Wiggler. The long thin foods could be represented by slim pirks, slim bar-spoons, unjointed Rapala-type plugs, Redgill style eels or other rubber eels and worms. The intermediates include devons, Tobys, normal bar-spoons, Hi-Lo or Runt type plugs, jointed Rapalas and so on. Not too difficult?

There is, of course, no rigid division between the types and usually the compromise solution will be the best starting point. For example, a Toby spoon or jointed Rapala is a pretty good sand-eel imitation and a *small* lure of any type is slimmer than a big one and may be mistaken for a thin fish.

However realistic the shape and action of your chosen lure it will not catch fish unless you can reach the fish with it – and having done so it will need to cope with the fishing conditions. For example, if the wind blows the plug back in your face or if the expensive spoon plunges to the bottom and stays there it will be useless. For each type of imitation it is useful to have a long casting (compact and heavy) version and a light (slow-moving) version. Also, forms which can be easily fished at various depths are almost essential.

All things considered, the aim should be to use a lure which looks and acts like the main food item of the predator you are trying to catch and which you can present within its range of attack. If you can achieve these aims then you must have an excellent chance of success.

INDEX

128